A CRACK IN THE WALL

A Crack in the Wall

New Arab Poetry

Edited by
Margaret Obank and Samuel Shimon

Saqi Books

British Library Cataloguing-in-Publication Data
A catalogue record for this book is available from the
British Library

ISBN 0 86356 329 5 (pb)
ISBN 0 86356 984 6 (hb)

This edition first published 2001

Saqi Books
26 Westbourne Grove
London W2 5RH
www.saqibooks.com

Dedicated
to the memory of
KPO
(Kenneth Pounds Obank)

Contents

8 Contents

Preface

The Arabic language remains the passionate pulse of poetic Arab expression, as it has been since earliest times when the arts of oratory and calligraphy were particularly revered in the Arabic-speaking world.

Because of its very close link with words both written and spoken, with the Arabs' love for declamatory language, and the arts of narrative speech in the common idiom, Arab poetry is not something apart from the general public. It is not the toy of a select and diminishing group of academics and professional writers that it appears to be in non-Arab lands. It belongs to everyone, for poetic idiom and imagery are the life-blood of the rich intricacies of music and meaning of the Arabic language, providing the reader and listener with a unique aesthetic pleasure that transcends class and country. These statements remain true of even the most "modernist" poetry in Arabic. The traditional links of poetry, art and music are still flourishing, finding new ways to say new things. Since the beginning of the last century non-Arab countries, particularly France and to a lesser degree Britain and the United States have had a significant cultural influence on traditional Arab styles and themes. Since the early 1900s young poets have gone abroad to study, Paris often being their chief centre of inspiration. There, as French poets have always done, they have experimented with metre and rhythm and rhyme, while remaining faithful to Arab temperament and attitudes to life. Lebanese and Egyptian poets were attracted by the French symbolists and their expanding of the range of subjects and treatments. Later, others were fervent followers of the Dadaists, surrealists and existentialists, and learned their special techniques by inspired translations of the works into Arabic. Many Arab poets today write directly in French.

The origins of free verse, so dominant in contemporary Arab verse, extend back to the 1930s. The poems in this book reflect that original enthusiasm for inventive poetic techniques. Women play an influential part in the popularising of fresh lyrical forms, and in the struggle for the recognition of women's equality in all walks of life as well as in literature. Men usually favour long-lined rhapsodical forms and mystical themes, often combining poetry with incantatory prose, sometimes ending free-verse compositions with a poetic prose section that can be almost indistinguishable from the surrealist and revolutionary lines.

That surrealist vein remains very strong, and with Arab utterance produces a sense of imminent danger or catastrophic change with tragic human consequences, a reflection of the political tensions and violence in everyday life. Some poets writing in this revolutionary style display great courage, and many of them live in exile, one of the major themes of their poems. Themes of nature and the elements, landscapes and city life form moving backgrounds to nearly all the poems. The desert, the sea, the sky, the sun, the stars are ever-present, with their attributes of sand, water (or lack of it), birds, flowers and beasts, inhabitants of time and space as enduring as the people with their passions, heartbreaks, jealousies and angers. There is a wide variety of themes in these works, from sexual passion and fantasy to maternal love and nostalgia for home.

As one of the translators, I must add that I have always tried to let each of my poets speak out with his or her unique voice. These voices sound so independent, aching with longing to be heard, to be understood and cherished, that it would be an impertinence to try to make them speak with my own poetic voice. Wherever possible, I have remained very close to the original texts in style and emotion, and even adhere to the poets' own special brands of punctuation.

I hope that these poems from *Banipal* will open up for the readers new vistas into contemporary Arab poetry, and that they will help to lead to a deeper understanding of the Arab soul, the Arab way of life, and Arab culture as a whole.

James Kirkup
Andorra, January 2000

Introduction

A Crack in the Wall is the harvest of the last twenty years of works by Arab poets of whom only a handful are known in the West. Here are sixty poets whose work is testimony to the profound changes that have taken place in Arab countries and throughout the world since the early eighties.

The poems are selected from the heart of Arab writing today. Readers will find them widely varied in style and that the poets write from all over the world, some from their mother countries, others having settled elsewhere – Europe, Australia, other Arab countries and the United States of America.

A Crack in the Wall is a selection of poetry from the 100-plus poets whose work has been translated and published to date in *Banipal*, the magazine of modern Arab literature that presents the reality of the modern poetry scene of the Arab world. It includes prose poems and free verse, both forms of which resulted from the great revolution in Arab poetry of the late 1940s and 1950s which broke through the classical traditions of form, metre and rhyme to establish the basis for the rhythms of free verse and, in particular, the prose poem forms.

But what is "free verse" and what is the "prose poem", the reader may ask. What is the difference? Certainly, in translation it is almost impossible to differentiate between the two. But in Arabic, the difference is very marked, the prose poem form having neither rhyme nor metric structure, while the free verse is liberated from the strict number of metrical units in the traditional classical line (*bayt*), but still bound by free metrical structures and rhyme schemes albeit unconventional ones. Among the poets who write prose poems are Sargon Boulus, Abbas Beydhoun, Waleed Khazendar, Amjad Nasser, Fadhil al-Azzawi, Qassim Haddad, Saif al-Rahbi, A K el-Janabi and Hassan Najmi, while those who write free verse include Mahmoud Darwish, Sa'adi Youssef, Mohammed Bennis and Salah Niazi. Readers will find no difference in the English translations between these two groups and those poets who write in English or French such as Tahar Ben Jelloun, Mostafa Nissabouri, Etel Adnan, Khaled Mattawa, Vénus Khoury-Ghata, Seema Atalla and Amina Saïd.

Our principal concern has been to show the quality of the poetry, the strides that modern Arab poetry has made since the days of that revolution in Arab poetry when Iraqi poet Badr Shakir al-Sayab, influenced by poets such as Keats, Shelley, Byron, Wordsworth, Eliot and Edith Sitwell, turned Arab poetry on its head by releasing it from the strictures of its long classical tradition. Last year, al-Jawahari, the last great poet to write in that classical form, died and with him the past truly became the past. But al-Jawahari was exceptional in that his subject matter was entirely contemporary – his poems concerned real life and human problems, exactly what young Arab poets are writing about today. With Badr Shakir al-Sayab came other great Iraqi poets, Nazik al-Mala'ika, Buland al-Haidari and Abdul Wahab al-Bayati, while before them, in the United States, Arab poets from Lebanon, Gibran Kahlil Gibran and Ameen al-Rihani, through the influence of Walt Whitman, had been developing forms of the prose poem.

The basis for contemporary Arab poetry was laid, therefore, through international literary influences. The works of T S Eliot, Ezra Pound, e. e. cummings, Charles Baudelaire, Arthur Rimbaud, Saint John Perse, André Breton, Guillaume Apollinaire and Lautréamont, to name only a few, have become part of an international heritage and consciousness handed down to Arab poets writing today, and particularly so through the magazine *Shi'r* (Poetry) founded by Youssef al-Khal and Adonis, with Mohammed al-Maghout and Ounsi el-Hage.

Readers of *A Crack in the Wall* will become aware of the vitality, the breadth of expression, imagery, and subject matter of these poets. The poetry in this selection shows an openness, frankness and willingness to look straight at difficult and painful issues and to face one's own limitations with humour. There is a thirst for life and the imagery is rich and startling, often with surrealist touches that bring the reader up short, confounding any stereotypes that a Western reader might, subconsciously or not, bring to bear.

Modern Arab poetry, for sure, is an essential part of the international poetry movement, bringing a fresh breeze of imagination, thoughts and feelings to the poetry of today's world.

Unfortunately, many poets are absent from this selection, poets such as Mohammed al-Maghout, Abdul Motti Hijazi, Fatima Qandeel, Zahir al-Ghaferi, Bassam Hajjar, Ali al-Domaini, Lina Tibi, Ghassan al-Khinezi, Ghassan Zaqtan, Rifat Sallam, Iman Mersal, Hassan Tilb, Ahmad Shahawy and Lukman Dairki. Translations of their work will feature in forthcoming issues of *Banipal*. We are unhappily unable to include translations of Adonis, Ounsi el-Hage, Saleem Barakat and Badr Shakir al-Sayab himself, since their works published in *Banipal* were written more than thirty years ago.

We are greatly indebted to every translator and poet for working with us so closely, and in particular to poet-translators James Kirkup and Khaled Mattawa, to Syrian literary critic Subhi Hadidi, and to German writer and translator Stefan Weidner who have read through the manuscript and made valuable suggestions.

We look forward to further selections and hope that many more Arab poets will find a receptive audience for their work among English-speaking readers.

The Editors
London, May 2000

Hoda Ablan

Hoda Ablan was born in 1971 in Eb, Yemen. In 1993 she gained a Masters degree in political science from Sana'a University. She has published three collections of her poetry.

Scraps

When he went away
I had nothing left of him
but myself

Corner

In a dark corner of my wound's room
I glimpse a shadow
two shadows
threads of shadow dancing with the needles of the fire
knitting the cold that lies at the threshold
I dress myself in it
and my longing shivers

Road

Barefoot, they run from their past
from hands waving behind a heavy wall
and trembling mothers who anoint themselves with a final
    tear
They dream
of garlands the earth will weave from the threads of their
    sweat . . .
and a road paved by God . . .
which no ghosts can close.

Uprooting

Why, when the wind sleeps
does an exile whistle through my clothes?

Starting

You are there, building a home
and I am here, demolishing a memory
Your home, which will be open to all
and my memory, which was open to your face.

Belongings

I had a house
a bed of dreaming wood
some pain on the shelf
a memory faucet
embers to sear my heart
whenever the cold assailed it
and many chimneys
but I had no door
and no window.

Mission

The bullet they aimed at our two hearts
so that we would separate at the point of blood
carried us to a room
on the seventh floor
of the university building
and returned safely.

Confession

Sometimes, at nightfall, I break down and cry
Then I resent my tears, which have illuminated the world
and extinguished me.

Hurt

To my brother Najeeb

Whenever I return to the playground of the past
peering into its deceptive spaces
I see your shirt, but not you
your smile, but not you
your eyes, but not myself
I meet, in what I find of you, the longed-for twilight
of when we were together
on the field of our dreams
and the warm blanket of my mother's stories, embroidered
  with songs.
Whenever I till the soil of memory
I find you, a stalk of grain aflame with tears
night's fingers snatch at you
alone, you face the wind
throwing into it all you have left.
Whenever I leaf through the pages of our footsteps
I find you hiding between the lines of the story
shivering in the chill of dreams
I drape you in the cloak of my love
shelter you from the bitter cold of distance
kindle your sorrow to warm us till morning.
Don't falter now
for the sake of your two new faces
they have already split away from you
and returned to the playground of the past
running
flinging open the gate of hope.

Spillage

I

My mother suspected that whatever was visiting me in my
   sleep would rattle the roof of our house
and that my heart was defiled above all else by love
so she poured my dreams into the street roofed only with
   accusations
refreshing the lungs of dust
but she overlooked two tears at the bottom of the bucket
which crept stealthily into her eyes
and have rained down ever since.

II

He poured his memories onto the floor
cities fell
faces shattered
all his hidden belongings bared themselves
the place which once glowed with oblivion has been defiled.

Translated by Seema Atalla

Fawziyya Abu Khalid

Fawziyya Abu Khalid was born in 1959 in Riyadh. She studied at the American University of Beirut, and at Lewis and Clark College, USA, and gained her doctorate at King Saud University, where she is currently lecturing in sociology. She has published three books of poetry, the first when she was 14 years old. Her poems have been published in a number of international anthologies. She has participated in conferences and poetry festivals in Melbourne, Sydney, Paris, Toledo, Manchester, New Jersey, and elsewhere. She has published three children's books, and articles on sociological research and politics. She writes a weekly column in the Saudi newspaper *al-Jazirah*.

Afternoon rainbow

Do I open my poetry book
or the valves of my heart
What poem could contain your small hand waving
at the school gate
What metre could bear the motion of your feet in my lungs
the jingle of your uniform as you cross the street into my
    heart
The noon sun sets your hair ablaze
Your chestnut hair sets the noon sun ablaze
with rainbow colours
You drop the heavy schoolbag from your small shoulder
like a branch unloading its burden of apples
and I hear the flutter of downy wings
You pull off your school shoes, releasing
a river of sacred ink onto the easel of my fortunes
You come closer, you leap . . .
Your kiss fills my veins with the restlessness of poetry
and the miracle of a moment as fleeting
as a wild foal

Umbilical cord

My mother drew from the desert
a string of sand
and knotted it to my navel.
No matter how far I go
I'm like a bucket
trying in vain
to scoop up the moon
reflected in the mirror of water
deep in a well.

Experiment

She mixed acid of ink with salt
of the sea and wounds of the soul
she mixed
she inscribed on callous desert
and merciful paper
wings and longings
she attempted to fly . . .

Cinderella

I hear the whisper of slippers in the clear air
one is on your little foot
the other tucked away in my heart
The charming prince's soldiers search
for two slippers, the one you wear, and the other, where?

Tomb

I feel cramped inside my body . . .
if I were to breathe deeply
my skin would split.

Water poem

She dipped her fingers into the desert
and wrote with mirage water a poem . . . that
                            drips
                            drips
                            drips
            a rhythm inaccessible to the senses.

First taste of death

   Deep in the vaults of memory
   a coffin gleams
   crowned with thistles and laurel
Who was that queen adorned with kohl and perfume
   whose legs flowed like a river of amber
   who lay unabashed across men's shoulders
as they carried her off and away?
   Who?
   Who was that queen?
   I prod my memory in vain
There's nothing but a vague pang of sorrow
   romping with insane insolence
   through the hollows of my heart.

Two children

For my mother Noor, poet, whose verses I borrow

I cling to her dress
as a child clings to a kite string
      I climb up her plait
as a squirrel climbs a hazelnut tree
Afternoons, we hop from one world to another
delighting in the air
like birds that have opened their cage door
We go from one game to the next
She teaches me
        names of flowers
        the seasons of rain
        love of our country
I teach her
        stubbornness and mischief
We share one apple and countless dreams
We make the desert into a paradise of questions
We splash each other with the water of mirages
        and befriend a stray gazelle
Dusk overtakes us
        In the obscure twilight
        who can solve
this riddle:
Which is the mother
and which the child?

Translated by Seema Atalla

Etel Adnan

Etel Adnan is a Lebanese–American poet and painter whose father was a Syrian officer of the Ottoman Empire, and whose mother was a Greek from Smyrna. Born and raised in Beirut, she studied philosophy at the Sorbonne and at Berkeley and Harvard. Settling in California she became an accomplished painter and poet. Between 1967 and 1982, years of devastating wars in Palestine, Jordan and Lebanon, Etel Adnan wrote her major (political) works of poetry and prose. Now she lives between California, Paris and Beirut and continues to write and publish poetry, short stories and essays. Her "love poems" have been set to music by the British composer Gavin Bryars. She wrote the French section of Robert Wilson's multi-language opera *Civil Wars* in 1984, and her play, *The Actress* (translated into English by herself), was performed in Paris in 1999. She travels widely for readings, lectures and exhibitions of her paintings. A bilingual poet and writer, she writes mainly in (American) English.

For Bob Grenier

Insomnia 1

1. Through. imaging.
   mountains even.
   water-eyes shut.

2. mirror. boxed in/
   production of one's
   light. (lightly)
   truck/load of. sweet
   night/mare with
   Faust.

3. trees growing on
   fables. legs parting

on linen. on hold.
Nebulous. love. of.
thoughts

4. tiniest of visions.
   an ⟶ gelic. fever.
   gulch. O C.a.l.i.
   f.o.r.n.i.a! Dimensions

5. blurrs. o no! not hiding
   mild. wild. kind.
   hind. . . fatigue leads
   ahead. ???????

6. Split. cloud.
   crooked effervescence.
   height of passing
   hour. un [yielding.]

7. the re/turn/rerun
   lived-in devil
   a throw of
   res/s/urgence.
   ex/haustion.

8. his/owl/on/
   the/ridge.
   ouuuuuuuh!

Insomnia 2

1. irreversible clarity
   over and why. stairs.
   whales eat water. when
   tears get married. to
   sea. the middle's middle.
   insomnia

2. women envy sailors
   as. additional. distraction.
   never colored.
   the police stands.

3. on a cyleByecycle. Auto
   nomous fear (roofs) the
   wind's hunger for repetition.
   two lines at a time

4. Funeral/s on two feet.
   to carry a light on
   one's back. Transparency
   of single thought.
   Dis/placement – care/fully –
   of. a. sentence.

5. Fusion of bodies.
   Fragility with marrows.
   Plus. Plus fanfare. napkins
   are maps. no food material
   traffic blocks desire
   on asphalt/ness

Insomnia 3

1. foam of Red Sea. Cat/ching
   Mercury. Lord of Time.
   visiting this room(?).
   Passage to: no/where
   fire's proportions

2. sun, moon, free
   what's . . . sleep?!
   ooooo! booooo. Darkly
   eyes. reversed.

3. lion. judgment of.
   indistinct/ness. Red
   with/in black/ness. O
   non/certitude of non/
   existence. The/re.

4. Break:up. down. over.
   through. So on and on
   until morning breaks.
   in. Ever.

March 2000

Seema Atalla

Seema Atalla was born in New York, completed high school in Amman, and now lives in Southern California. In 1992 she received an MA in comparative literature from the University of California in Los Angeles. Her translations have appeared in *Méditerraneans*, *Passport*, *Prairie Schooner*, *Painted Bride Quarterly* and other journals. She writes in English.

Zaytoun*

The olives of America are round and rubbery.
Jammed into jars, they gasp against the glass
like hungry fish.
On your plate they loll about hollowly,
having no pits.
You know by their name they will pass through your palate
swiftly, like a short vowel,
slip like an "l" from your tongue, leaving no taste.
Sliced, they may sigh
through the spaces in their middles:
Olive . . . O live . . . Oh, live!
but they will not come alive.

The olives of Arabia are different:
they won't let you forget.
Green beads squinting through cross-slit eyes,
sharp Calamatas with inky points,
wizened Aleppos that stain the fingers with flavour –
all of them greet your teeth with a seed,
stay your bite with an "ay",
leave souvenirs.
They hum on the tongue with the zest of a "z",
linger like long vowels.
Pressed, they will ooze

---

* *zaytoun* means olives.

with the oil we call *zayt*,
murky and marvellous.

Ten years here.
I am losing the words now.
Ailing, I cannot cure
the olives on the trees I see.

They ripen unsavoured,
like the words I've stopped saying.
I find them
strewn on the sidewalks like an alphabet
familiar and foreign as the language I left
on my mother's tongue.

Holy Land

For my grandmother Melia

Head
bent in the heavy
halo of lamplight
stitch by tiny
stitch
how patiently
you occupied
the evening

Painstaking
such delicate detail
precise
the perfect petals
vines entwining
leaf by tiny
leaf

(Besieged by sudden
borders)

Settlements sewn
to the hills
bases secured
with double knots
checkpoints pinned
to the perforated
fabric

Calm
in the cornered crook
of a sofa's arm

Land spread flat
in that holy glare
altered
by invading needles
villages picked apart
old roads
unravelling

Melia
counting the careful squares
within confining lines –
surrounded

The scarlet skeins
and veins of your hands
fill the grid
cross
by cross
with piercing
colour

Fadhil al-Azzawi

Fadhil al-Azzawi was born in 1940 in Kirkuk, north Iraq, and started publishing his poetry in Baghdad and Beirut when he was 15. He acknowledges an enormous debt to the cultural diversity of Kirkuk where Arabic, Assyrian, Kurdish and Turkish were the mother tongues spoken. He has a BA in English literature from Baghdad University, and a Ph.D. in journalism from Leipzig University, and has edited literary magazines and newspapers in Iraq and abroad. To date, he has published in Arabic seven volumes of poetry, six novels, one collection of short stories, two works of criticism and numerous translations from English and German literature. His poetry has been translated into many languages; in 1997 his collection *In Every Well a Joseph is Weeping*, translated by Khaled Mattawa, was a winner of the US *Quarterly Review of Literature* international poetry book competition. He left Iraq in 1977 and has settled in Germany.

Feast in candlelight

Here is the twentieth century
in its long dim hall
with murderers and conjurors
sitting at its table
in the flickering candlelight
of their victory
waiting for their meal.
The waiters come out
one by one
from their hidden corners
balancing dishes of darkness
on their heads
to serve their guests.

They will all drink from the same bottle
watch the evening fall among the trees.
Parades of drunken soldiers
wave their bloody flags

and march down the street.
Through the window
the moon will soon shine.

When they finish their feast
we will sit at that same table
and drink the same wine
too.

I want to change myself

After all my heavy losses
here and there
after all my ever-bleeding wounds
from the lost wars of my short life
I saw how fragile I was.
I sat and thought about what I should do
to rebuild the ruins of my afflicted soul.

I think I have to change my body parts
one by one,
some of them, at least –
no matter what the cost is –
to earn the happy days to come.

I think I need
a new pump for my heart
to love as many women as I want.
I'll need a lung, washed out of tar and nicotine
to smell the streets after rain,
and nerves of steel
to bear the blows of fate,
and new blood, rich with red and white blood cells
to donate
to the war victims in the Balkans.

I need
a stomach that thankfully digests all I give it,

sharp teeth to tear the barbarians
coming down upon us from their snowy mountains,
a wide chest to be kind to treacherous friends,
long limbs to win the Olympic Games,
and tender lips for burning kisses.

What would it matter if I were bald?
My remaining hairs
the wind will gently comb back.

My liver and spleen
I will leave as they are –
I really must spend as little as possible –
and my head will just have to find its way
out of trouble the way it has always done.

In short: I have to be alive enough
to write a love poem like this one
to still look like myself after all.

Listen, Noah!

Listen, Noah!
With our feeble arms
we've built
newer and higher embankments
against the coming floods.

Whenever a ship sank
the carpenters built another.
Memories of the future alone
kept our hopes alive.

Through the centuries
we heard the wailing of the drowned
everywhere.

Our miracle:
we always survived.

The Wise Men in our house

Misguiding the thieves
creeping about at night,
we hide the Holy Spirit,
with its gouged eyes,
in the refrigerator.

On the wall we hang seismographic charts
and chatter about Einstein and his black holes.
We sit in the kitchen and smoke;
heavy water mixed with peppermint
boils in the kettle
while the blind goose that lays
golden eggs
is roasting in the oven.

The Wise Men have come at last.
Salima says, "I'll make
an angel's breakfast
for our guests."
We change our places and go
to the living room,
and wait for our coffee.

Living has become really expensive;
all these hypotheses only to measure
the light curve,
all these victims to win a single war,
all these pharaohs only to ask
for a mummy's hand.
Nobody talks about all that now.
Nobody cares for others
because there is no proof of anything.
What is positive is also negative
like every hope, like every doubt.

Oh, so many mysterious tribes wandering
among these empty galaxies.

In a garden, in a distant garden,
we lie back under alien stars
and remind ourselves of our happy days
in paradise.

Bedouins

Three Bedouins in a desert,
carrying sacks strapped to their shoulders,
walking one after the other
stooped for eternity
like defeated soldiers.

Three Bedouins in the desert
walk on silently
as the wind blows now and then
and wipes out their traces.

Events

Something always happens:
a war can be declared suddenly
a baby born in a cave
a lonely heart broken.

Shall I forget all that?

Something always flows:
water in a river
wine in a tavern
tears and blood too.

Can I stop all that?

Something we always miss:
a sentence we learned by heart

an umbrella forgotten in a bar
a woman with whom we fell
passionately in love.

Can I be happy about all of that?

And if nothing happens –
if I do not win a million pounds in the lottery
or find a treasure in my garden
or I do not take a trip to the moon,
for example.

Should I not be sad then because of that?

Go, Fadhil, to Heaven, and thou, al-Azzawi, straight to Hell

On the way to Heaven
on the way to Hell
I saw a dozen prophets
with long hennaed beards
gathering gems and pearls for me.
I saw angels
spilling like evil souls
through the cracks of shattered dawns.
I saw Bedouins running
along greedy shores
feeding their dying embers
with my eternal fire.

Launching my scream
I held these sluggish caravans
starved and lost
and guided them
to their promised land.

On the sea
as my boat twisted its prow

through huge waves
rushing from the horizon,
the desert's black bloated clouds
showed me the old warrior's path
sloping down to the plain of shadows,
and I went on.

Along the way
barbed wire stretched before me
and life sang
her joyous melodies
to vanished pyramids.

Oh, who knows if the sand
will ever remember me
in this everlasting exile?

Within the broken heart of earth
under twisted, riven rocks
the darkness grew and grew.
The bloodstained spears of my forefathers
pierced God's purple skin
deep into the scales of the creeping serpent
and stabbing once, twice . . .

Wandering in the heavy rain
of prehistory
I lived and hoped
to reach another shore, new and green.
But the cunning storm thrust
its sinnewy arms
thundering,
and dragged my broken boat
into the bleeding abyss of history
giving me in its second whirl
dizzy once more
with the blessings of amnesia.

O treacherous ages, I forgive you!

Long and desolate is my road,
to all those distant planets
between the Little Bear
and the Big Dipper.

Come, Fadhil, come.
Let's begin our journey again
to the city of Heaven, of course.
As for thou, al-Azzawi,
go straight to Hell.

Translated by the author and Khaled Mattawa

Basheer al-Baker

Basheer al-Baker was born in al-Hassaka, Syria, in 1956. He has published poems in several Arab literary magazines and in 1995 published his first collection. He lived in Beirut and Tunis before settling in Paris in 1986, where he works as a journalist.

from Lamps for a European sidewalk

1

No country, no woman, no money,
nothing but the soul roaming about like a lonely ant,
a heart carbonising like a flower of morning despair,
rooftops of sadness stretching along a horizon of failure.
Orphans and outcasts,
this is an age becoming extinct.
And as you read the maps of your country
the remains of a chivalry scatters about.
If you were in Paul Eluard's place
you would have let go of the past.
You would have let it drift in the winds of an old future.
No home,
this is the freedom of capital
where the child goes to sleep with his machine
and broadcasts words of loneliness.

2

No country, no woman, no money.
And how does the old country show itself?
Will it buy a first-class ticket
to come to this long drought?
Will the women come waving their Italian hats
exposed like forbidden fruits?
And will money reach you
as you stagger under the debts of the past?

3

No country, no woman, no money.
For a long time we have walked along the edge of the cliff
touching women's fingertips in late summer
as if these drinks held the scent
of womanhood and our departed country,
as if these new mornings can lead us to a distant yesterday
when we played in small lagoons
and spent time betting against failure.
Long long years, and we are still there
listening to the murmurings of our souls
withering beautifully like ageing sea birds.
The scent rose, but it never reaches us.
The evening twiddled its fingers, but never came near.
It was a distant carnival that lived in dirt, rivers and
    childhood,
and now wears the clothes of a late anguish,
a soft death.

4

No country because walls of despair rise out
of the grass of small evenings.
No woman because the pomegranates of the fields
are further than the river channels,
because trains and suitcases
are more delicious than a single tear in the dark.
No money because the sea went on rising
until it reached the neighbour's windows
and took over the bedside stand.
What can I say to a kiss as it slides
from the lips of Mademoiselle S
with the softness of an unfettered night?
What can I say to the wound as it howls
into the urns of Mademoiselle J's speech?

Translated by Khaled Mattawa

Ahmed Barakat (1960–1994)

Ahmed Barakat was born in Casablanca in 1960. In 1977 he started publishing his poetry in Moroccan and other Arab newspapers. He published two collections of poems before his sudden and early death in 1994.

Another idea

That is possible only in one case:
all that surrounds us
not in darkness
but in wakefulness, and under the whip of light

Sunset

The animals that closely resemble the clouds
The dark cloud that looks defensive like a billy-goat
The slain billy-goat now at the gateway of another evening
The other glasses of fire
Those that the sky in the west gulps

And this man here who cannot now see
The fish commit suicide on the high seas
And this man here who cannot now hear
The whispering of ants on the lower deserts

Surely the animals that closely resemble
The dark clouds
Will embarrass him.

What's happening to me is terrible

Forest! Where can I take all these branches cut from the
    trees?

The sun is setting
The woodchoppers are still shouting at their axes
And I don't know, forest,
Where I can take all these branches cut from the trees!

The anthem of cruelty

Nobody has asked me about you, dog.
I no longer encounter anybody, not even that philosopher
who once introduced me to you and then departed.
Besides, nobody talked to me about you, dog.
Don't keep looking at me with brotherly eyes
Don't keep panting before me as though you were a
    defeated army

What do you know about me, dog?
Do you want me to sing on your behalf?

Message

Going shopping
Please wait for me
You can do your laundry if you're bored
if the door bothers you remove it
and replace it with anything
Please don't leave your face in the mirror
as you leave by the window
Don't commit suicide as is your wont to do
but wait for me.

Translated by Hassan Hilmy

Tahar Bekri

Tahar Bekri was born in Majel, Tunisia, in 1951. He started writing poetry in 1964, in both Arabic and French. After his release from jail in 1976 for opposition to the country's single-party regime, he left Tunisia for Paris, where he gained a doctorate in French-language North African literature. He has published ten collections of poetry, six limited editions of poems with paintings, and three books of essays on Tunisian and North African literature. His poetry has been translated into several languages. He is a member of the Tunisian Writers' Union and in 1993 he was awarded the Order of Cultural Merit by the Tunisian Republic. He lives in France and lectures at the University of Paris X at Nanterre.

from The impatient dreams

He loved the swallows flying over the sea
and did not know why,
rain and wind hoisted his sails, from
war to war, he told the wild roses of his
wrath, the horizons carried his footsteps towards
oblivion, the bruised sands destroyed his lost footsteps.

Fisherman of stars, he discovered satellites,
the sky like a motorway, humans like
crazy seagulls, here the planet shakes
its volcanoes, there it stirs its rivers for help,
in vain the ocean replied to its call.

Old ocean, as you used to say, Lautréamont,
but I never listened to you, he cried to the lost sun,
the heart like a brazing fire, the desert which encroaches,
he built dams against the fleeting moment, the seaweed
stole away his dreams, there on the quay of his pain.

And the earth burdened down with its wounds
shrouded the light, he strolled through

the oak-tree-lined paths of memories, on and on,
at times the spiders concealed his view,
the cemeteries full of their dead leaves, without pity.

Days carried his silence
in the echoing woods, words snatched
from tempests, this country is mine, he used to say
to the misty mornings, yes, Jalaleddin Rumi,
the world is like a flake of foam!

The silver birch bark hardened its knots,
a thousand dry herbs for a spark, all
these wasps are not worth a bee, the sea rye
for an offering, the expectation of evenings
hastened his peace, already the night
in the heart of torment.

Like flocks of indifferent birds, the cries
carried on without stop, the echo in the masts
sawing his fervour, the oars thrown against the sides;
to wander (did he remember) as an ivy climbing up to
the windows, little by little, the doors closing again,
on themselves.

He opened the book of the sea, tireless,
the words had just died on the banks,
wave after wave, he woke up their race,
horses of fire, letters trotting, there are, said the friend
orange trees which die of sadness.

I see, Hamlet, dead bodies piled up
like logs for a huge fire,
vultures, old desert, and abandoned bones,
alongside my thirsts, my head crying out for dew,
and these poppies which never leave me.

Translated from the French by Claire Farah

Tahar Ben Jelloun

Tahar Ben Jelloun was born in Fez, Morocco, in 1944. In 1971 he went to live in France with the ambition to be a film-maker, but turned to writing. He writes in French and has published numerous works of fiction, poetry, criticism, and essays on current affairs, particularly on issues of racism. He is a regular contributor to *Le Monde* newspaper. In 1987 he was awarded the prestigious French literary prize, the Prix Goncourt, for his novel *The Sacred Night*, and in 1994 the Prix Maghreb. His works have been widely translated.

from The raising of the ashes

This corpse that was a body will no more stroll along the
    Tigris or the Euphrates
scooped up on a shovel that will recollect none of its pain
shoved in a black plastic trash bag
this corpse that was a soul, a name and a face
returns to the earth of the sands
detritus and absence.

This earth avid for water has had only blood to irrigate the
    great silence
this desert of affliction has laid open the trenches of sleep
    and men in their thousands have been engulfed by them in
    a flash of torn skin
a lighted candle kept vigil within the defunct ribcage.
A shred of sky inhabited these corpses destined to oblivion.

A coverlet of sand has been disposed on these black bags by
    a hand of iron.
No more movement. Not even the fulgurant memories of
    first loves.
Nor the unknown bird flown from far-off day to the prayer
    for the dead. It is black, unmoving, eyes scorched, eternal.

This body that was a word will no longer think of Homer
gazing upon the sea.
It has not been extinguished. It has been touched by a flash
of sky smashing word and breath.
These crystals mingling with the sand are the last words
pronounced by those unarmed men.

Faces blackened by a flame that does not waver.
Page of a life charred to impenetrable secrecy.
The gaze, slowly torn from the face – is a thin sheet of paper,
beautiful but tough, disturbingly light; a veil between our
life, our death; a silence harbouring a few grains of sand.

Faces washed by the same brief, effective fire are no longer
faces.
The sketch of a remembered face is dumped in the same
black sacks.
Disorder and defeat have muddled days and appearances.

This body that was all laughter
is now burning.
Ashes carried away by wind to the river
and the water receives them like the ghosts of tears.
Ashes of memory adorned by a very simple little life, a life
with no history, with a garden, a fountain and a few books.
Ashes of a corpse reprieved from an unmarked grave and
offered to the tempests of sand.

When the wind rises, the ashes will go and lay themselves
upon the eyes of the survivors.
Who will know nothing of them and
they shall walk in triumph with the touch of death on their
faces.

Innumerable are the signs releasing their waters
in extremities of tumult
there, at the edge of a moving cemetery.

In this country the dead travel
like statues and like flames,

they wear eyeglasses
and hold out their fire-scorched arms to fly away.
We say they became invisible
and go to offer the living the years left them to live.
Thus the desert is strewn with so many years: a century or
　more.
Lives to be taken like stuffed jackals
lives that tremble as they say:
"Death is not as fatal as are night and shadow to the sun."

This body that was a dream is a devastated dwelling.
It has neither door nor window
just a lacerated mattress, a pan, stale bread, a coat
hung up, walls blown out, grey dust and last year's calendar.
Eyes are holes where the flies are nesting
the mouth is a wound
and the skin no longer remembers anything.

Guests have arrived, saying: "War is no excuse!".
But the house is no longer an abode,
it is absence and silence.
On a strip of wall
the dictator's portrait is still intact
flies cover it with their droppings.

The charred trees
go on standing
When the wind shakes them,
shrivelled birds fall out
No child's hand picks them up.
Covered with dust, they roll among the thorn bushes.

That's how the desert is.
Suffering brought into a town
or into a mountain village.
From such a land comes an ochre rain and a wind bringing
　bad news:
"Ahmed son of Ali has offered up his soul for his country. A
　martyr, his body cannot be brought home. He nourishes
　the earth . . ."

He who is wandering today in the sleep of others
is not a martyr.
He is a tree of ashes
a vessel without armour
a blind statue.

A voice rises from a dried-up well
it comes from a century far far away
when Babylon was prayer.
In those times the world could never die
children said: "The world is suffering but it will never die!"

There is beauty melted in earth
a city
the skeleton of a city
seated in an archaic
hospice where straw corpses come to die.

Baghdad has no more stomach
she has opened her veins
for a people who go hungry
On its forehead the portrait of a gravedigger is intact.

From this sky so white
falls a funeral mask
a voice:
It is our destiny at stake even if we wish to remain
    anonymous.
But the earth compels us; it swallows us then vomits us into
    the river's brackish waters.
We float on our backs, bellies inflated
eyes staring at the sun
we no longer have eyes, but empty sockets that hold images
    captive.

Our skin is no longer our skin.
They fleeced it from us like a stolen robe
like a borrowed shroud.

The scorch-marks creep like the memory of our tears
and we are bereft of all that is merciful.

Is it a storm or is it the picture of our defeat that is being
    drawn in the streets?
Vanquished, we are no longer ourselves
and our heritage is the abyss.

Another voice:
I shall not say we
because I want to vomit
but I no longer have a stomach
I no longer have a body
I am a sack
a jute bag filled with earth
I am a field at the cliff's edge
I am a field of stones where serpents are sleeping
I feel the cold in my separate limbs
is that what hell is
feeling cold in a phantom body?
Who speaks from the bottom of this grave?
Me?
I no longer exist.

From another grave, another voice:
I fell asleep. Naked.
My feet wearing the army boots of death.
I was expecting glory
and it is words covering our skin
Words
mouldering of unmoving time.

I fell asleep in other bodies emptied of their entrails
they were still warm
the thing moving there is not an arm
it is a famished cat struck by lightning.

Our words have fallen into the grave
they are no longer words
but a gluey sperm in mud and shame.

They tell me: our own mourning is in the look children give
    us.
Who shall tell them the story of our defeats?
Will they believe us?
I see them spitting on the faces of the dead
so many useless words.
Ah speech, words, the litany of the starving
bitter bread buried in the lowly earth
I see them running to pick up our scuffed shoes
they make a bonfire with the poems written by the generals
and inflame our memory.
They no longer spit
They no longer speak
They forget . . .

Ephemeral childhood

They have immense eyes devoured by trachoma and
    oblivion
Born out of season, they run through the alleys like shafts of
    light
who will lend a shadow to these bodies treading scorched
    earth?

In a paper boat they sail
dressed in palm branches and leaves.

There is a sadness, at evening, that descends the scale of time
    and covers their brows like sweat.
Do they know?
Their eyes forever widening
they are stamped with the washed sky
they move over the reeds they whip.

With their impatient dreams
they make misfortune tremble.
Beauty lies between their teeth like death

an immense burst of laughter
a tear on the faces of mothers.

Childhood and innocence are left to the world's fraternity
    and to the ants
laying ephemeral stars on the cemetery
they speak to the dead and displace the stones whose
    memory of exile they become.

24 April 1986

It is a village beyond time
where men and stones are motionless
where the ewes and the mules stand waiting.
The grass is scorched by the snow
a lame shepherd is looking for a tree on which to hang
    himself
clouds broken by the rays of a mocking sun
descend and take the place of hills
the mountain lies close to the sky
it will not move.
"You must learn to forget" says a voice.
Men, stones and beasts have nothing to forget.
Here, the first season of silence watches over an old horse
    with glazed eyes.
The days fall like drops of icy rain
suspended between the dry branch and the earth.
Men no longer know how to count
they dream of dying as they say their prayers.

1990

Translated by James Kirkup

Mohammed Bennis

Mohammed Bennis was born in Fez, Morocco, in 1948. At the age of 20 he started a correspondence with the poet Adonis, who published his poems in *Mawaqif* magazine. His first collection was published in 1969 and the most recent *Nahar bayna Zinazatayn* [River between Two Prison Cells] in 2000. He has written numerous essays, and a four-volume work on modern Arab poetry, and translated many literary French texts into Arabic. He was editor of *al-Thaqafa al-Jadeeda* cultural magazine until 1988 when it was closed down by the Moroccan government. Since 1980 he has taught in the Faculty of Arts at Rabat University, and in 1985 he co-founded the publishing house Editions Toubkal. He was also the driving force behind the founding of the House of Poetry in Morocco which opened in 1996, and is currently its president.

from Hieroglyphics

1

A ghost
you attend to the ruby time
No east will rise in you
or west
A niche
drowned in blue rustle shrouded by the Kingdom
A clay horizon
Eternity
dangling like a bunch of grapes
for a hand that drifts away
and dies

A stone
forgets its master
Was he
here
or was he there
A stone above a stone

rises to watch you
the Comer
No one
is still awake but you

A silence attends to me
And for you
my guest there will be a night of papyri
and a night of
ageless
distances
arriving in hissing scents
The night's end
and beginning
are identical
Friezes are becoming one
under the feet of the river's dusk
Intoxication echoes resonate inside me
and fade away

2

You may follow me my guest
You may choose the trips
with me
as an arch vanishing
between one confusion
and another
as a flock of setting windows
You may extend yourself like an attack
and open up for me
a trough claimed at once by the tyranny of Desire
and the edge of the sword
My body
dweller of the guest's garden
tell me about the boat of the sleepless
half of the sun
that shrouds the dead with the shadows of its gardens
so they can watch her blood
being realised between a fate

concealed by words
and stars that keep the memory of darkness
My body
a river that covers me with spectral birds
incite the scents of ghunbaz, the native plant of Fez,
against the night's heaves
Petals
that dew drops
repeat
their openings
Stones of flight
Two hands
on the edge of something
which I cannot name

incite your shimmers
inside their lineage
so every tomb
is certain
of its scream
angles of light
cross thresholds
that are swept away
by a heavenly leaf
and surroundings
whose scorching is sweet
and by rubies of wandering

**and I have a house there exactly
where an illusion is reflected on
the slopes of its awakening so
will the linen bandages fall and
eyes crowd in on my limbs
fro and fro an inner light
completes the anguish of tension
slow forgetfulness is born
whose days blindness rescues
a scent has the horizon of
meadows as if missing
its own evening**

6

and you are the guest and here's your season the
wreath falls naked between the crystal and its hardness the
book won't inherit a supplication the dead pledged
to you an opulence overflowing with wings
and then they crowded in on the stairs of splendour

For the horror to guarantee the glitter of the night's winner
who cloaked in cracks descends
          My gift to you
                    my gift to you

is my master the Flame the zodiac tells me
Inkwell
Tablets
A chair overlooking the birth of a lake
drowning out the hymns a voice telling the Scribe
to lightly write what's steeped in silence astonishing
others write blots that turn into roses
whose glow is multiplied in secret

And go gentle
on this guest
Oh
my body

7

Two gracious hands
To what beginning have I granted my blood

Slow down if you get closer
and if
you get closer yours
is the dust

Nothing falls down from your hands
except what they
sipped
from the clouds
The corners of the earth
share with you
the flint-stone of the storm's saps
A slice of eternity reveals to you its bereavement
A sun defends
the lacunae of the Book
   your hands
        your hands
Compare what's poured out of your hands
with a glowing ember in whose sources creation finds
a groove of gentleness

Are you
by yourself
or
are these birds
coming back from the saffron clusters
through the ears of wheat
guided by a disaster
honed
by flint
and
earthly remains

Rose of dust

1
Shattered places
and the breeze
of dawn wakes up on me

2
My shoulder still in slumber
A cloud bowing
to the flicker of infinity

3
Is it that trees invent their echo
or
has the blind one
just dipped his hand
in water

4
The poet closes
his eyes
on a rose
of
dust

5
Scratching my window-pane
the pine tree
lightly shudders
under a snow of ashes

6
Smooth water
From which paleness
did the wind return
and throw another topaz in the river

7
Solitude
could
end with winding paths
intoxication
trips
But whenever I inquire about death
a lady stands against me
impetuous and mute

8
The night barks here
Thumps somewhere
And I am drinking
Hölderlin's wine

9
A shimmer
Then another
Enough for the magician
to make sure
that time is tame
that poetry is a call

10
No one saw me
quietly opening a drawer
to see
where did my self
sneak in

11
My bones have their own biting frost
Is there a name that will go out
before me tonight

12
Clouds upon clouds
flutter
A leap
I almost thought my hand
was made of clouds

13
Play with my poetry's lock
I say
I'm a lantern
a rug
a snow
a wall

14
Two stars kidnapped my hand
For a second
I watched it
tremble
weep
Am I
or am I

Translated by Anton Shammas

Mohammed Bentalha

Mohammed Bentalha was born in Fez in 1950. From 1979 to 1981 he was general secretary of the Union of Writers. He was one of the co-founders of the House of Poetry in Morocco and, in 1999, co-founded the League of Writers of Morocco. He has published three collections of poems. He is now professor of literature and chair of the Department of Arabic at the Ecole Normale Supérieure of Marrakech.

Nakedness

When he'd devised a saddle,
and twice tested it, fitting it on a marble horse,
he was wearing a necktie,
trousers,
and his beige torn socks;
he did not pay any attention to those who slandered him;
but, beginning to speak, he recoiled,
bit his lip,
dozed off
and fell fast asleep.

A smile at the bottom of the scale

A rose in one hand. The other hand turns the pages. Who then slipped on their eyelash between the book and the dice board soon after the author's outing to the Pigale department stores? The author said: the river has the affection of mothers. He was gazing at the surface of the Seine, hoping to see live sharks. But all he could see was the reflection of bells and the ships moored on both sides. He returned home. He stared at the clock on the wall and turned towards the wardrobe. His socks were gyrating to the jazz tunes coming from the lounge. The old hats were doing to the LP what the female slaves would do to the lady of the château before her lover arrived. And from a wink, they made a scale for laughter.

King Henry was there.

And they would plan some practical jokes: in St Denis, they would exhibit their charms in exchange for a volume of poems, and he would write two drafts. In a tavern at the back of rue Mouffetard, they would entice him, sometimes with orations, and at other times, by winking at the customer sitting in front of him. But he would get embarrassed.

He would then take the crown off and place it on the customer's head.

Transition

When in the depths of the *nahawnd**
I burned
my sail,
this passionate parchment went blind.
The star then turned to coal,
and the echo in the pastures to grass.
O reed flute, cut from the rock
as my arm was immemorially!
How has the coal become a star?
And how has the cloud
become my sail?

Translated by Hassan Hilmy

---

* a basic musical key in Persian, Turkish and Arabic music.

Abbas Beydhoun

Abbas Beydhoun was born in 1945 in Sh'hur, South Lebanon. He studied Arabic literature at Beirut University, and later at the Sorbonne. He was a Marxist activist for many years, and was arrested and jailed in 1968 and 1969, and again in 1982 during the Israeli occupation of Lebanon. He started writing at an early age, but only turned singlemindedly to poetry in 1974 after a break from writing of seven years. He published his first poetry collection in 1982. He has been arts editor of several major Arab magazines and newspapers, and is now arts editor of *al-Safeer* newspaper in Beirut, and a literary and art critic. He has published ten collections of poetry, the latest in 1997.

A man without burdens

I enter another person's life the way I enter a street. I map its facades and alleys. When I leave, it remains long and dark behind me like those fathers who always watch me from a distance without hurrying to begin my birth.

Three peaks disappear behind me. That is why I keep meeting people I cannot recognise. And when I feel a bird coming from the opposite direction, I realise how rarely this happens in this land without wind.

They are dead, probably, but they can still inspire me. I, the one who promised only to live. I pick memories and dreams. I churn them again into the cold earth where I live among my fears.

I live on plugged springs, and by the water that yellowed at my birth. Since my life disappeared here, I have been following fishermen's tracks. I meet strangers and I move in the twilight that trails their lives. I do not do this in any shorthanded way. But with the betrayal of a single man, maybe they will stop running from the fear that chases them. The inner doors of the sea may open, because a man has hardly lived, and now he arrives without burdens to be born among them.

Vermeer's wall

The small crack in Vermeer's wall may be what is hurting me now. Too often we abandon ourselves to cracks like this. I think it originates in a kind of recklessness: you live with a suspicion without paring its nails. You see a comma and refuse to consider that it will become a painful &, and you continue to think that caution will not result in more walls. You spend so much time with ephemerals that you find your life without a ladder to climb.

The small crack in Vermeer's wall that disappeared may have been a lie to begin with. Pain is only a signature, and we speak long after the signing.

The flower of life and my father's black heart

We ate live secrets,
the flower of life
and my father's black heart.
I ate them;
they had no taste
except that my hands
tossed away a heap of lies
that never flowered.
My hair grew empty and seedless
and I threw a fistful of names
to the birds
but they did not care.

Dreams and potatoes

They put the fish in the oven. They pull dreams out of the earth. Here where the people of the well were lost, others too disappear following bird tracks. We grubbed for dreams and potatoes and we plucked live fishes. We ate many secrets and many more springs. Until the pyramids leave us, we will not mind the earth that has fled our eyes.

Five

I gather around my fingers
thoughts and pedigrees
but the number of my fingers
remains the same:
five buried in mud.
With my toes
I make an inlet for speech
and a small "A" blocks it.

A wave

The wave, as it rolled, did not notice it had lost its calling and that it was going back to being a gasp. This happened when the sea was nothing but depth. Those who played on its surface never noticed the wave's absence. The light water that was about to disappear pulled us further in. Touched by a strange breeze, we never stopped dreaming of sails. When water recedes to being only a smell, we move on and note here and there an earthquake clearing its throat. With the power of hearing alone we found even older chronicles. And when our tracks are lost, higher levels of silence will disappear, and stones that were about to catch their first scent of life.

When we direct our smiles at other depths, they follow us without stopping, and the child-volcano smiles above the surf.

from Rooms

1

And I say goodbye to these stones
that have begun to ramble
and have blackened all at once,
those stones we skipped over as we ran.
We will not say the wind was also foolish
when it blew over them.
The sea will lick them;
this will always happen.
The sea licks them
and the air sniffs at them endlessly.

2

Rain falls without a care
on my life
which is always lit like a jail cell.
I leave it now,
where only a door remains to me.
I did not always live here.
I had my friends' homes.
Since that night
I stopped being the gardener of my life.
A wicked vine
grew among the grasses,
and no one weeded out the follies
whose roots have hardened.
I am no longer the gardener of my life.
I leave it for new tenants and friends
who earned it with their betrayals.

3

Rain falls too
and the earth is slick under its brush.
The stones are shiny with the saliva of the sea.

The day is smooth, bald
with the sleek laugh of the sea,
and I, sleepless on a hotel bed,
gaze with an empty smile at the sea.

4

Goodbye to the fort
they razed two generations ago.
They still wander about where it stood.
Goodbye to the asphalt,
my longer hair,
to the song I drank from a Russian novel,
to the radio that broadcast a life
that never came my way.

5

We were ill
like our hoarse homes,
a little sick like our animals.
Our houses were behind the world
where waters yellowed before our birth.
Our rags and the rumblings of our coughs –
we pushed them out further
along roads made of our wheezing
and threads of urine,
and we traveled on their backs.

We lift our heads
from the knee
from which we emerged.
We fumble by our fathers' ankles,
and the months of their illness
are split among the towers of our lives.
We turn stones over,
and that fire that follows us like cracks in the road
reminds us of the dilapidated light
where they spun their wheels
with the same slowness
that steered us to sleep.

We too broke away
from where the roof was rent
leaving the rooms to rise like calves
and give birth to us again
as strong shoulders bend on
readying for travel.

6

This house from which I pulled my stake
totters without falling.
My father and his friends
leave under their own shoulders.
After they healed the wounds of their absence
they stayed here
under the roof that has remained low
and the curtain that has been yellow
since that time.

Air does not blow from unknown places.
It is here and will not leave
like a shirt they took off and left.
The shadow that has remained on their pillows
delayed the coming of that morning
and stands until now
hesitating by the staircase.
And the lantern,
a line of smoke and a line of perfume
they left behind,
is the light that clings to the cliff edge,
still in service
since it was dimmed
by their beds.

Their long illness makes stones blush
and paints them with the smoky colour
of an invisible liquid.
It may have disappeared
but it is still encrusted
in shirts and curtains
as if starching them.

It has lived among us a long time.
And even after gathering it repeatedly
it remains alive like an elixir
and delays their departure to infinity:

The farewell that has gone on
until it never happened,
and the death that came and found nothing.

7

On these sombre stones we fell,
and there life started.
Maybe we fell like stones
from the light of those rooms.
Or we emerged glistening like worms
from the saliva
that has remained
dry on our skins.

There was a handful of a scent,
always in the bottom,
a smell like that of buried nests
that we step on without noticing,
a smell of cows and sex
that passed ahead of us.
Here, whenever we step,
we feel it bleeding under weeds
and we sense it
still holding us there.

We die under cooking clouds
and the smoke of sardines.
The sea that rises in its overflow
smells of blood and salt.
The earth is skinned at the start of rain;
its hot liquid covers us in sleep.
And this stable that has suddenly risen beside it!
We leave from the bath of moonlight
without noticing

that the redness that has tanned us
will not soon disappear
and that we have built a great sleeplessness
for our skin.

Limasol, 1986

They

I sit surrounded
by those
who made me
alone.

A sketch

The boats are drawn on the water,
and the water does not move
fearing them.

Translated by Khaled Mattawa

Faraj Bou al-Isha

Faraj Bou al-Isha was born in Libya in 1956. He went to teacher training college and worked as a primary school teacher, later turning to journalism and writing. He left Libya for Cyprus in 1988 and, with the poet Fatima Mahmoud, established *Modern Sheharazade*, a magazine concerned with Arab women's issues. He published his first collection, *Qassa'id* in 1987, and two more in Cyprus (1992 and 1993). He lives in Germany now as a political refugee, and writes for the London-based newspaper *al-Sharq al-Awsat*.

Where does this pain come from?

where is it leading to?
I pick at my wounds,
like a nomad spurring his donkey
impatient to reach
the end of the century.

Here I am

tossing at your feet
the knowledge I have gained
from my mistakes.
I waited for your arrival
and picked at my soles
for meaning.
What good is this step
or that step?
This is how
I became stranded
in the mud of modesty.

Wait

do not leave yet.
Let me rearrange the world
for you.

Sleep

the doves have subsided
the tiger slouched
and the ox now ploughs.
The camel tossed its rider
dying of thirst
and went on its own.
Sleep
the snake dreams of another poison
the ghoul has devoured
the children of fantasy
and my grandmother
has made a pillow
of the tales we loved.
Sleep
the earth is your palace
and your terrace
is the seventh sky.

Translated by Khaled Mattawa

Sargon Boulus

Sargon Boulus was born in 1944 in al-Habbaniya, Iraq, into an Assyrian family. He started publishing poetry in 1961, contributing to *Shi'r*, the modern Arab poetry magazine of Youssef al-Khal and Adonis, then working in Beirut on both *Shi'r* and later *Mawaqif* magazines. He settled in San Francisco in 1969. He has published five collections of poems, his first *Al-Wasool ila Medinat 'Ain* [Arrival in Where City] in 1985, his latest [*If You Were Sleeping in Noah's Ark*] in 1998, and some short stories. He has translated many British and American poets into Arabic, including the work of Ezra Pound, W. H. Auden, W. S. Merwin, Shelley, Allen Ginsberg, Sylvia Plath, Ted Hughes and John Ashbery. A biography, written in Assyrian and Arabic by Robin Shmuel, was published in Baghdad in 1999.

Master

Some leftover champagne
with dead bubbles fermenting in a glass.
Our party has come to an end.
Last year has vanished
in the catacombs of the past
as if it never were.

On the edge of the glass: a fly.

Someone says:
This century is almost over.
Perhaps another master
less cruel and dumb will come
to open a passage through this wall
or at least show us where the new road
would begin. Maybe we can change.
Tomorrow we will rest.

No, the other one says.
Tomorrow we will assassinate
the new master. If he ever comes.

Entries for a possible poem

Outside
it is suddenly dark

Above the church tower
night opens its thousand eyes

The village surrenders
    to the awe of
        stars

In the corners
        of the room
phantoms struggle
        defeats are many
conquests galore

Stretching his hand
    he switches on
        the table
            lamp

The notebook is open
    on a few sentences
        mostly scratched out

Last night's
before-sleep scribbles

Sketch of a face
whose owner he cannot recall

A woman with a gazelle's
                terrified eyes

Storm of apprehensions
flowering into fever

he picks up the pen
  and, feverish, writes:

This evening,
  this evening,
No, it's already night

Back from my usual stroll

The village
at this hour –

A fat lady
  with a small dog
who would always greet me
   very sweetly
    Guten Abend

 sometimes
a drunken farmer
  dragging his feet
at the end of a carnival

The thin saint
  who guards
   the ancient steps
 of the Gothic church
with a long pole
  and pointed hat
sometimes looks
  like my father
   in his late illness
   silvered
    by the stars

Did you notice
 how many there are

In my childhood
we slept on the roof
my father taught me their names

I live in this village now
   The stars are almost the same

Somewhere else
     (very nearby)
     somebody is bombing
     a sleepy village
identical to this one right now

Many years ago
    this very one
     too, was bombed
Not so long ago – mine

On a night like this
sleep is hard to come by

I should go out
   and see the stars shine

    for one last time

On a night like this
   in an age like this

    Wisdom
 is a form of despair
silence too often a crime

Better to cancel
all tomorrow's appointments

Not to answer the phone

Instead of seeking an answer
    find the Question

And for once
    expose the Lie.

Schöppingen, Germany, March–April 1999

Remarks to Sindbad from the Old Man of the Sea

Are you already tired?
Our quest has barely begun.
Forget the sea.
Stop dreaming of ships and trade
I'm the last voyage you will
ever make, and likewise
was the first.
Every way
you came by,
every road you took,

I paved with my own hands
for your sake.
and you still complain!
Too heavy on your shoulders, you say?
That's because
I carry eternity's weight
plus my own, and need your legs
to take me around
in my journeying
between night and day.
You will try to escape,
I know, time after time;
you will dream every night
that you crush my head
with a heavy stone
and dance drunkenly
over my corpse.
But if you happen to venture out
into those woods alone,
night will only deepen
around you, in every whisper
you shall hear
a hissing snake, poison and trap
will be your lot everywhere.

Don't try to escape.
Forget the sea.
Stop dreaming of ships
and trade; today you have unbound the knot
of my waiting, and from now on
you will carry me on your
strong back, Sindbad,
to explore this island together,
you and I, I and thou,
as one.

Who knows the story

The century is almost over;
How did it start, when will it end,
against whom is this battle being waged?

Since it began: From the first chapter. Before speech.

Those who stayed behind,
read the writing on the wall.

He who migrated, never found the promised land.

Speak, what will you say?
Or don't speak, and just listen.
Listen to any voice that may reach you.

Toss your old key into the ocean
as long as: no lock, neither a door, nor a house.
Visit our forsaken land sometimes.
The magic ring you covet is to be found there.

The woman you sought after, to no avail,
for so long, awaits you there, now.

Open your hands. Auction off your heart. And hear the
  story.

The day is coming; countless are the signs.
The people ask for bread. The tyrant sees a dream
that defies interpretation.
The peddler of fatwas, purple-clothed
with the blood of sacrifice,
rips through the luxurious fabric of your dreams
with a dagger of righteousness
beating his little tabla all through the night
between your ears – his ultimate joy:
that you never sleep.
The deadlier your migraines, the higher he soars.
It is a world clouded with mysteries.
Mysteries are embedded in words, but
what they tell is only one part of the story.

The audience believed it.
The judge was suspicious of the details.
The scientist thought it was a dance:
between particles and monkeys and trees.
Between the seed, the ant, and Mars
and the galaxies whose giant arms
embrace a cloud of dust.

Don't speak; what will you say.
Or speak, and listen
            to whoever comes along.

The Chinese poet
        dead more than a thousand
years ago, whispers in my ear;

> "From this high tower,
> I am startled to see
> how ferocious is the storm.
> The walled city looks empty
> when the leaves fall."
>   *Li Dong*

Maybe it's the wind, Master Li Dong,
reciting the story of the flood once more.

My tribe knows it well.
It knows its master and narrator.
It knows its heroes, those windmill shadows
Don Quixote fought valiantly
once upon a time: today
the coughing of a sick child
without medicine behind the walls
of siege, is enough to make it fall.

My tribe. This page. This pen. This wall.
It is the sap, Master. The sap rising
in the trunk of life and the tree.
No. It is the sea of silence, and this
tiny boat has a story.

My friend who died yesterday in exile
battling his final pain,
knew the story from beginning to end
in a single moment of yearning.

Let the current take what it wants.
Let me remain in my place.
Give me this single moment, and let me be:
I want to hear the story.

1998

Mahmoud Darwish

Mahmoud Darwish was born in 1941 in al-Barweh, Palestine, and grew up under Israeli occupation. He lived and worked in Haifa, editing *al-Ittihad,* (the newspaper of the Israeli Communist Party), and becoming the best-known Palestinian poet in the world, a symbol of the Palestinian people, subjected to house arrest and prison. He published his first collection of poetry in 1960 and his latest, the nineteenth, in February 2000. In 1969 he was awarded the Lotus Prize, and in 1983 the Lenin Peace Prize. He went to Cairo in 1970, and then lived and worked in Beirut until 1982 when he settled in Paris, writing there two of his most acclaimed collections. In 1981 he founded the literary quarterly *al-Karmel*, which he still edits, now from Ramallah. The English edition of his book *Memory for Forgetfulness*, an odyssey of a single day in Beirut during August 1982, was published in 1995. In his last two collections, he moves away for the first time from being a public symbol. A new French anthology of his work *Poesie: La Terre nous est étroite* was published in March 2000 by Gallimard.

Without exile, who am I?

Stranger on the bank, like the river . . . tied up to your
name by water. Nothing will bring me back from my free
distance to my palm tree: not peace, nor war. Nothing
will inscribe me in the Book of Testaments. Nothing,
nothing glints off the shore of ebb and flow, between
the Tigris and the Nile. Nothing
gets me off the chariots of Pharaoh. Nothing
carries me for a while, or makes me carry an idea: not
promises, nor nostalgia. What am I to do, then? What
am I to do without exile, without a long night
staring at the water?

Tied up
to your name
by water . . .

Nothing takes me away from the butterfly of my dreams
back into my present: not earth, nor fire. What
am I to do, then, without the roses of Samarkand? What
am I to do in a square that burnishes the chanters with
moon-shaped stones? Lighter we both have
become, like our homes in the distant winds. We have
both become friends with the clouds'
strange creatures; outside the reach of the gravity
of the Land of Identity. What are we to do, then . . . What
are we to do without exile, without a long night
staring at the water?

Tied up
to your name
by water . . .
Nothing's left of me except for you; nothing's left of you
except for me – a stranger caressing his lover's thigh: O
my stranger! What are we to do with what's left for us
of the stillness, of the siesta that separates legend from
   legend?
Nothing will carry us: not the road, nor home.
Was this road the same from the start,
or did our dreams find a mare among the horses
of the Mongols on the hill, and trade us off?
And what are we to do, then?
What
are we to do
without
exile?

Translated by Anton Shammas

What we needed was a present

Let us go then as we are:
You, an unfettered woman

And I, a true friend.
Let us go our separate ways together
Let us go exactly as we are – united
And divided.
With nothing causing us pain:
Not the divorce of doves nor a chill between the hands,
Nor wind blowing around a church.
Almonds blooming, but not enough?
Smile then and let more almonds bloom
Between two butterflies – your dimples.

Not long now, there will be another present.
If you look back, you'll only see,
Behind you, places of exile:
Your bedroom
The courtyard willow
The river behind the buildings made of glass
And the coffee-house of our rendezvous. All, all
Are turning into an exile.
May we be well!

Let us go then as we are
An unfettered woman
And a friend, true to her music.
We aren't old enough to age together
Making our weary way to the cinema
Witnessing war's end between Athens and her neighbours
Or observing the peace between Rome and Carthage.
In a little while
Yes, in a while the birds will migrate to another time.
Was it a path made of dust
In the guise of a meaning, that led us on
A journey between two myths?
There must be a path, and we too must be –
A stranger reflected in the mirrors of his stranger
"No," you say, "this is not my path to my body.
There are no cultural solutions to existential concerns!
Wherever you are, there my true sky
Will be
And who am I to bring you back an earlier sun and moon?"
May we be well!

Let us go then as we are:
An unfettered woman in love
And her poet.
Not enough snow has fallen
In December? Smile then and snow will fall
Like carded cotton on the prayers of the Christian.
In a while we'll return to our tomorrow, left behind
When we were young, there, at the beginning of love
Playing out the story of Romeo and Juliet
To learn the vocabulary of Shakespeare.
Butterflies have fluttered out of sleep
Like a fast-moving mirage of peace
Crowning us with two stars
And, between two windows,
Killing us in a conflict over the name.
Let us go then
And may we be well!

Let us go exactly as we are:
An unfettered woman
And a true friend
Let us go as we are. We came
With the wind from Babylon
And to Babylon we are travelling.
My journey was not enough
To make of the pines on my way
An utterance of praise for the southern place
Here, we are well. The wind is
Northerly, and southerly are the songs?
Am I, the man, another you
And are you, the woman, another me?
"This is not my path," you say, "to the land of my freedom
This is not my way to my body
I would not be 'I' twice
When my yesterday has taken the place of tomorrow
And I've split into two women –
I'm not a woman of the East
And I'm not a woman of the West
And I'm not an olive tree giving shade to Qur'anic verses."
Let us go, then.

No collective solutions to personal concerns!
Being together was not enough?
Let us be together then.
What we needed was a present, to see
Where we are. Let us go then as we are
An unfettered woman
And an old friend
Let us go our separate ways together
Let us then go together
And may we be well!

Translated by Ibrahim Muhawi

Drought

This is the hard year.
Autumn did not promise a thing
and we did not wait for prophets to appear
and the drought is as it was before:
A tortured land
a gilded sky.
Let my body be my temple.

. . . And you must reach the bread of my soul
to know yourself. For there is no limit to me.
If I wish:
I will widen my field with a spike of wheat
and widen this space with a turtle dove.
Let my body be my nation.

Autumn still stares at the river,
or gazes toward the trees
and overlooks my deep well.
There are no limits to me with you . . .
The sky is faithful in autumn.
Imagine, if only once, that you are a woman
to see what I see.
My body is my master

and autumn is as it was: Whenever
an idea dries up, the choir of devotees
blooms: Water, and water.
What need have I of prophecy? Kind angels
are guests at the dreamers' cloud.
What need have I of your book
as long as what is within you is within me?
My body unfolds into itself

and autumn bids farewell
to the seven dry years
and the city now must have its peace.
There must be goats nibbling at the grass
rising from the Babylonians' books or others'
for the sky to become faithful.
Light up my darkness and my blood with your wine,
and live, with me, in my body.

Translated by Khaled Mattawa

from The Damascene Ring of the Dove

1

In Damascus,
doves fly
across the silky fence,
two
by two.

2

In Damascus,
I watch my language,
letter by letter,
being inscribed on a single grain of wheat,

with the needle of a woman;
then refined by a Mesopotamian partridge.

4

In Damascus,
the barefoot sky
walks the ancient alleys.
Why would poets need
inspiration, metre, or rhyme?

5

In Damascus,
the stranger
sleeps upright, upon his shadow,
like a minaret upon the sheets of forever –
he doesn't miss his homeland,
or any one, for that matter.

10

In Damascus,
a deer
sleeps next to a woman
in a bed of dew.
Off she takes her dress
and shrouds the river.

11

In Damascus,
a bird pecks at
what's left of the wheat
in my hand.
She leaves me a single grain, though,
for her to divine my future, tomorrow.

14

In Damascus
I introduce myself
to me:
Here, in the shade
of two almond eyes,
we fly like twin birds;
our past deferred.

22

In Damascus,
the traveller sings in secret:
From Damascus I won't return alive
or dead, at all;
I'll return as a cloud
that takes the butterfly burden
off my wandering soul.

Translated by Anton Shammas

A cloud from Sodom

After your night, the last one
of winter, the seaside promenade
was empty of the night-watchman,
there was no shadow to pursue
my steps, after your night had dried
in the sun of my song. Who will
tell me now: let go of yesterday,
and dream freely in total abandon?
My freedom is near, it sits with me now.
It perches like a familiar cat
in my lap, and gazes up at me,
at all that you've left me from yesterday:

your lilac-coloured scarf, a video tape
about dancing with the wolves,
and a string of jasmines to lay
over the moss-covered heart . . .

What will my freedom do
after your night, the last one of winter?
"A cloud went from Sodom
to Babylon" a hundred years ago
but its poet, Paul Célan,
committed suicide today
in the Seine.

You will not take me
to the river again. No watchman
will ask me: and what's your name today?
We will not curse the war.
We will not curse the peace.
We will not climb the garden's fence
looking for the night
between two willows and two
windows, and you will not ask me:
when will peace open
our castle's gate for the doves?

After your night, the last one
of winter, soldiers pitched their camp
in a distant place, a white moon
settled on my balcony, and I
sat in silence with my freedom
staring at our night.
Who am I?
Who am I after your night
the very last one of winter?

Translated by Sargon Boulus

Mohammed Dib

Mohammed Dib was born in 1920 in Tlemcen, Algeria. He was educated there and in Oujda, Morocco. He began writing poetry at an early age, also to paint. He worked as a teacher, accountant, and interpreter, and in 1951 became a designer and journalist on *Alger Républicain*. He went to France for the first time in 1952, where, between 1952 and 1957, Editions Seuil published his trilogy of three novels. In 1955 he signed the manifesto *Fraternité algérienne*. Seuil published his novel *Un été africain* and Dib was expelled from Algeria by the colonial authorities. In 1964 he settled in France, where he still lives. He has published numerous novels, collections of short stories, books of poems and children's stories. He published his first collection of poems in 1961, *Ombre gardienne*, three in the 1970s, and major new collection, *O vive*, in 1987. His latest collection, *L'Enfant-Jazz*, was published in 1998. He writes in French.

Garden

Garden sleeping black
And sometimes sighing.
Nothing but black
Sounds in the darkness.

And the house itself,
All given over to night,
Black outbuilding.
Yet still there and

Moving on, halting.
Starting off again
Soundlessly, again halting
Waits, listens perhaps. Listens.

Bent over the trees,
Over the house, the night.
Not a word spoken but
It surely protected.

Something come from afar
And black too, trying
To recognise, to see
The world with its hands.

Tree

Tree waiting.
Then it got dark.

It stayed there.
The child watching it.

He said: it's night.
That said, he went in.

Dinner. Staying up late.
What about the tree? he said.

The child asked himself
under the lamplight.

The child whose eyes
The tree came and closed.

The window

At first
Down there
A door opens.

And further on:
Another one.

And further on:
Yet another.

Then further on again
A window.

Opening to the sky
And two heads were seen.

Two children's heads.
Two sticking out.

The moment

That very moment
And the moment after,
No war, no dead.

When people open
Their eyes and fall asleep.
Wherever flowers grow.

However much they're loved,
However lovely, near or far.
Their look never changes.

The wolves

He lay down in bed.
But the door. The boy
Saw it was shut.

He ran to open it.
Ran back to bed.
Quickly pulled up the sheets.

Then waited for death.
With closed eyes he died,
Dreamed of a woman in grey.

She came in to make a fire.
Suddenly wolves entered
And sat around the fire.

And a bitter smell of fumes.

Forward march

A voice shouted.
The child turned around.
He fell into step.

Came only to the wall.
Turned and marched back.
Found only the wall.

Turned half right.
Found only the wall.
Turned half left.

The door opened.
The voice still shouting.
His soul was white.

Shoot

Through the window
He took aim.
With his trigger finger.
A man fell dead.

The street did not move.
Silence did not move.
The sun did not move.
The sky watched the child.

Child with trigger finger
Took aim at it.
It did not move.
The child fired.

Translated by James Kirkup

Nujum al-Ghanim

Nujum al-Ghanim was born in 1962 in Dubai, in the United Arab Emirates. She has published four collections of poetry. She has a B.Sc. in video production from Ohio University, and an MA in art in media production from Griffith University, Australia. In 1980 she started working as a journalist, writer and producer for UAE radio and television, and from 1985 until 1999 was editor of the arts pages of *al-Ittihad* newspaper in Dubai. She now works as training co-ordinator for Abu Dhabi television.

Rain

Today the sky cloaks herself in grey,
lifts her new umbrella over her shaven head,
and girds herself with water.
A fine lady, parading in a dress like an icy waterfall.
Meanwhile, lovers cheat on their wives
and children run away from their mothers
firing the pistols of their eyes into space.
            And the trees,
even the trees bow down
to the unexpected touch that will restore to them
            the cup of life.
Today is like love's first kiss
time and again we anticipate it, like waves, or a pool
drenching the body and stealing its scent.
Today I spread out letters and poems
and sit expecting the call of the meadows
            that put us away one morning
        and have not woken us till now,
            while outside the rain drowns the streets
            caring for noone.

So I'll arrive late

Why is it
whenever I shake the past
off my shoulders
its sun descends on me,
beating down on my head?
I ask the water,
the passers-by,
the children setting out early:
Why do you follow me?
There's no loaf in my basket
to pull out after dismounting,
no match
to light the darkness,
not even a handkerchief
to wave in surrender.
I ask the gentle rock,
the dry, haughty branches,
the few lights remaining
behind distant curtains.
I ask
so as to evade these memories
and occupy myself with finding
another way home.

Blue lightning

I emerge from the day
to be devoured by lights.
The city leads me astray in its labyrinth.
I emerge disoriented
so that the crowd nearly crushes me with its enormous
    shoes.
I look around:
the faces are stony,
the voices disappear into my ears leaving no trace,

bearing no affection.
Faced by the harbour water,
I shiver as though stepping out into the open air.
But the stores are bustling,
and so are the boats lying chaotically along the quay.
My hands gesture
but my tongue is tied.
Should I return?
Drive the flock home to sleep?
Open my tent to the late-night fires
and draw out the thread of speech?
Or search the damp and foggy alleys?
Here I am
        eyes reprimand me, tongues rebuke me
till I fade into the hubbub
shirking from the streets.
I hear an intriguing moan in the alley,
the roads draw me into their maze,
the dark blue trees with eyes
all over their branches
pursue me in the darkness
and the illuminated signs splatter the passers-by
with strips of colour.
The place is redolent of ginger and arak.
Longing shadows me
keeping track of my comings and goings.
I catch sight of the walls
within which I'll collapse,
but before entering my room
I'll look to the heavens to cleanse me
from the dust of these terrifying apparitions.

Translated by Seema Atalla

Qassim Haddad

Qassim Haddad was born in Bahrain in 1948. He worked for a number of years in the Directorate of Culture and Arts at the Ministry of Information, but now devotes his time solely to writing. His first collection of poetry was published in 1970 and to date he has published sixteen books (eleven poetry collections and five books of prose), in addition to *Majnun Laila*, a limited edition volume with Azzawi of poetry and paintings. He was a co-founder of the Bahrain Writers' Association, established in 1969, and an editorial consultant of their literary periodical *Kalimat*. He writes literary criticism for several Arab newspapers and magazines, and lives in Bahrain.

Words from a young night

1
We are not an island,
except to whoever sees us from the sea.

2
Wine in half the cup,
the other half was not empty;
it was lost in ecstasy . . .

3
To write
is to breathe unused air.

4
They delighted in sleeping
because of the treasures it lay
between their eyes.

5
I write about love
the way a child draws his impressions of
adulthood.

6
An impossible dream
is kinder than a rampant delusion.

7
The curtain on the window
is an orderly more powerful
than his sultan.

8
A vessel between water and fire,
an enticement for flames.

9
He counted his friends to me
on the fingers of his hand.
Then I realised
that his hand had no fingers.

10
To rule = terror to force acceptance.
To dissent = terror to force resistance.
Both seek to grant prosperity to the people
under one power.

11
I am not free to accept.
I am free only to oppose.

12
I see the wind playing with the flag
of this place,
while people go without air.

13
A space crowded with answers.
Everyone is besieged with answers.
Answers in every corner,
and in everything
there are questions.

14

He wants to apologise,
not because he was an enemy
but because he revealed himself as one.

15

Pigs are useful too.
They sing about the garbage bins.

16

She is like the state.
She puts on her make-up
and talks to her mirror,
and never listens to people.

17

All this night
is not enough for my dreams.

18

Every day
we do nothing but confirm the futility
that has been impossible to detect.

19

Usually
I let my memory graze on its own . . .
To forget the wound and remember the knife.

20

The future
is said to be the opposite of the past,
and we are in an endless present.

21

I have many secrets.
I study them in my poems
and I toss them in the air of language.
Someone has to expose them.

22

This person I do not know
and who does not know me,
why is he so late in arriving
leaving me
to the loneliness of the sidewalk?

23

The children grind their teeth,
and grind with their hearts.

24

Night,
you are not alone.
There are countless other hermits.

25

I look at them;
they are ready to change their stances
by simply shuffling their shoes.

26

They meet for dialogue
and they exchange points of view
the way they exchange masks.

27

Silence . . .
is a flagrant accommodation of folly.

28

You will not convince him with words
if he is not convinced by reality.

29

Before you sleep
place a rose on your chest.

30

What is the difference.

between someone blind
and someone who does not want to see?

31
The clicking of my chains fills the place,
I,
who claim freedom.

32
My lips tremble now before a word . . .
My lips are defeated.

33
Be prepared . . . the past is coming.

The friends there

Friends
weave their new rags
in a morning with a missing sun.
Their bodies convulse, and their fingers are caught in a fever
of work.
They spin language with the excitement of magicians and
the confidence of artisans.
They offer wool to summer, and ice to winter.

Friends east of the water,
they work well in solitude.

I stand on the shore.
I watch their silhouettes outline the horizon.
I send them books in bottles that expunge my words,
and they are exceedingly gentle with them.
They run on a bridge
with flaming feet
and there
they climb, burdened with scrolls,
a bridge that praises geography and disparages history

and vigilantly watches against the written word.
They hold texts under their arms
and descend like goats decorating the road.
I embrace them.
They cross through terror.
Their memories are of blood,
and their fingers, fastened to glass shards,
are soiled with hacked hearts.
We crash in the midst of love and death
like waves churning salt and luring vessels.
Naked bodies of young men,
where a shirt is never woven for summer,
and no feast is prepared for winter.
The lonesome friends are there.

Body

I saw you in a body where stallions moan
and from whose arms storms emerge.
Abandoned to sighs
trampled by fillies with the whinnying of desire
and the infatuations of mating,
words issued from you like a reed tucked
between sadness and steel.

I saw you among a murdered race
storming with fire and broken glass.
A body raving with love,
a soul neglected by death.

Translated by Khaled Mattawa

Nathalie Handal

Nathalie Handal is Palestinian-American. She was born in 1969 and now lives in Boston, USA, and London, where she is studying for a Ph.D. at the University of London. She has an MA in arts and creative writing from Simmons College, Boston. Her poems have been published in many literary magazines, and in 1999 she published her first collection, *The Neverfield Poem* (Post-Apollo Press, California), and also brought out *Travelling Rooms*, a CD of poems to the music of Alexandr Alexandrov and Vladimir Miller. She writes in English.

Roof tops

The roof tops cry
           the squirrels hide
the breeze circles around the light tree
and I see the color of your eyes in the corner of a leaf.
The marching of deaf warriors, the clicking of broken
heels, the roaring of a faraway chimney, the missing
piece of an unknown flag, the bees and the yellow drops
falling on your fingers, fingers stained with the message
of a cigarette you smoked a while back, and all is gone now
except the stains have memory and the wounds even greater
memory for the desert comes in their dreams, reminds them
that the river left, forgetting to tell them why . . . forgetting
    that
the ruby was under the table we use to lean our elbows on,
    the table
which knows more about our hearts than we do, knows
    more about
the confessions of our hands but the greyness of this Parisian
    sky
has stolen the tablecloth, and yet behind impossible lines
    and cracked surfaces
there remains the innocence of a silence, too silent.

The roof tops cry
>   the squirrels hide
the breeze circles around the light tree but
there is no light, no tree . . . there is no breeze
the color of your eyes though, remains . . . in the center of my
  mind
like the bird which will never leave the secret fields of
  myself
like the whistling of a train I once heard, that comes back to
  me
when I think the stars have healed the crimes of the night
  and discover
that I will never forget the faint trembling of that hand and
  that cigarette.
The roof tops cry, we hide, the breeze circles us . . . will we
  ever arrive?

Escape

Time escapes us and gives us no time to escape
Voices caught in the narrow distance between two rain
  drops.

Times escapes and gives us no escape
and we continue listening to the rumbling of passing
  travellers,
the slope of our tragedy ending with nothing but bare hands,
memorising the journey . . .

The blue jacket

The stars' dust falls on the shoulders of the blue jacket,
and as it slides down to the end of the sleeves,
finds a place at the tower of my fingers.
I let the asterisks discover the heart of the sheet

and allow the ferries to travel wherever seaweeds and
    lanterns call them.
I think of the love song in the back pocket of a martyr,
the way he continued to walk slanted until the end of the
    smoke
and remembered the white and yellow pack of cigarettes
    sitting in his shirt pocket.
I knew that I could find hiding colors in the curves of
    branches
but all the colors I wanted to see were in the blue jacket.
Subways and wargames were afternoon attractions for those
    who survived,
but I still lived by the blue jacket's rules, after all, its threads
    healed the bruises on the child's feet
and hid the only arak bottle left from the invaders . . .
The blue jacket, I continue to wear it, so that I can remember
the day I saw him in dew drops, the day small ivory thorns
    found refuge in envelopes
of letters going . . .

Mohammad al-Harthi

Mohammad al-Harthi was born in al-Mudhayrib, Oman, in 1962. He has a degree in geology and sea sciences. He has published three collections of poems, and writes on travel in Arab newspapers. He lives and works in Muscat.

Pawns of sand

The drowned remained
in their bottled dimness
and the moon drifted
on its course.
The ironed djellabas
also kept waiting
for their lives
which the hunt
had taken to a gathering
dusty with preys.
And the crow
    who with his eyes
had bled a feather
    that neglected
to place a horse
    in the grassy landscape
couldn't find
    a new trick
for landing on trees
or even just a colour
that can still muffle
    the sound of
    falling leaves
in a hall filled
    with shadows.

No one came
    to their aid

They didn't exchange
the pawns of sand
or half-words
with which to wet
     the camels' glances
and nothing else
     happened as
        well.

Because
     they just
waited for all
     that time
until they were dead.

At a slant angle

You were not
the meanings' cohort
or its opposite,
but between two doors
you paced with half-words,
you scaled the roof of dream
with the fabled
adventure, stalked the arm
and cane that became
a road, as evening fell
in the elegies and
the mirrors.

Nor were you alone
as you went down the slope
of your life where
you weren't alone.
Your hand lit the candles
of air, the dawn's photograph
wove the morning haze
with a sleepy needle

and a morningless woman's
       lock of hair
in the immense mirror
that reflects the same image
with a slant angle
       at the end of the slope
you never understood
       was your life
            itself
hung at the entrance
          to paradise.

Translated by Sargon Boulus

Mohammad Afif al-Hussainy

Mohammad Afif al-Hussainy was born in Amouda, Syria, in 1957, into a Kurdish family. He has published three collections of poems and a novel. He has lived in Sweden since 1989. In 1999, he established, and now edits, a Kurdish cultural magazine in Arabic, *Hajalnama*.

Shadows

Where are they from,
these shadows,
secretive as the graves of relatives?
We sent them small bouquets, and afternoons
spread shadows over the days.
Below, in their magical country,
are men we call ancestors,
in the neighbourhoods of the dead.

My brother

He was fair-haired.
He used to sleep early
and wake early.
One day he left us quietly
just as he came – quietly.
He was my brother.

Names

We seemed like willow trees
our shirts woven with tales.
Suddenly we found our way into

the black frames of the dead,
exchanged places with them
and with the coldness of the glass.
The tales died too
and our blue names turned yellow.

A flower

How sad was the candle of distances
and captivating expanse.
Distress robed the golden domes in its shadows.
The steps flickered in the stealing shades of sunset,
and near the grave of Olaf Palme
he plucked a yellow flower for the dead,
gave up his sadness to the core of the place.

Death

Those few who waited for our death
never said they missed us,
never sent us chronicles of their lives.
Nor did they write to us,
as though forgetting we are dead.
Since we crept from their letters
we created for ourselves the rustling autumn.
Now it is up to them to make ready
the vacant seats deep within our souls.

The benches

The benches are cold outside.
Neither a lover sits on them
nor a rose in full bloom flowers beside them.

These benches are very cold in winter.
They teach themselves to be patient
like old memories of the dead.

Glass

Does the window and its broken glass recall
how the wind swept against it?
Does it recall how the children nearby
fought with the sunset?
Does the window recall it is abandoned,
tainted by absences and accusations?

Translated by Noel Abdulahad

Abdel Kader el-Janabi

Abdel Kader el-Janabi was born in Baghdad in 1940. He left Iraq in 1971, and settled in France after living for a while in London and Vienna. He has published a number of volumes of poetry and essays, and translated works of Miroslav Holub, Paul Celan, René Daumal, Joyce Mansour and Max Jacob into Arabic. He has founded and edited journals, *Grid, al-Noqta*, and *Faradis*, a serial publication *Arabie-sur-Seine*, and a magazine on surrealist literature. In 1998 Actes Sud published *Éternité Volante*, an anthology of his translations of Ounsi el-Hage. His anthology, in French, of Arab poets, *Le poème arabe moderne*, was published in 1999. Janabi translates and reworks his own work from Arabic, as he did with the poems below, except for "Hat trick with rapid" which was written directly in English.

History always wants to refer me to you, André Breton

These lines are dedicated to the bandits of the windy city

André Breton,
windows are open
and your becoming is eyed by their curtains.

From under the blanket of unapplied thought
I see you holding a dream
curved between your hands
a phoenix smeared with blond haze rises up
and gives you a sultry look
for you are handsome like "a militant swan"
whose tongue is wading into my enemies' mouths.

Your smiles are indications of flames
foresights which permit
civilisations to melt into celestial bodies
streets in which to pile mobile corpses
and flowers to bleed the four corners of the air.

There is no bird curious enough to fornicate with a wood
The old-timers are of no consequence.
To furbish their sobered call
they kneaded the tongues of a horizontal insomnia
they are priest-ridden dogs
the needle of death is their phallic symbol
and I should say
you have to go down on paper
loaded with a growling anguish
to be hurled into the bedrooms of their visions.

But you come to me never with what they know.
For I see you a woodfire butterfly
cleaving cascades of knowledge
blazing running water
whose depth is a shape of elsewhere
an epicurean domain engraved on the stone of flesh
with fingers comparable
to the interior convulsions of uneven sounds
Then I see you "touching only the heart of things"
like a limpid nightfall
that tiptoes into my wide-awake sleep.

You "hold the thread"
and still I see a curious childhood
stronger than death
weaving invisible sands
implanted on the shores of sleepless mirrors
where the gesture of insurrections
sings its reincarnation.

The poem is a being
and History – the hive of ironies – is in no hurry
to see that a windy city
is reserved
for your springs.

Willingly, the light

For Paul Celan

Of other Israel
I'm gonna talk
of the Western Wall
of the Old Testament
which paved the road
of Shulamith with ashen hair
drinking the black milk
in the nightdom of the Word
of a camel
I'm gonna talk
was lying down there
stars flashed above him
like a pair of scissors
that has wandered through the mind . . .
of this man in the house
I'm gonna talk
and of those serpents
when dusk falls
of the jackals
of Kafka
and of the far north
which brought a new fact
in the Temple
the day after
the surrogate body of the lost
was being resurrected in the effulgence
of black ponds.

Every sea has a boat to immobilise it

For Pierre Peuchmaurd

We were children in search of happiness
happiness in search of children

we were the antithesis of a world
a lightless world
a slopeless mountain
we were a golden fleece
the mob couldn't reach
we were the voice
and the poem
the morning
and the light
the head
and the practice before the game
we were the white-haired revolver
in the worker's hand
while the bullet
was down there
in the heart
fumbling
between the lines
for words.

We were howling
like a hurricane wind
settling the score
that History will beam
from the exquisite corpse
and shower
over our graveyard.

Hat-trick with rapid

For Salah Faiq

Behind every scream of subtle alterations
of a dark rain falling from the dreamer's eye socket
of words your mouth dropped on the bed's edge
of a tobacconist murdered by a cloud of smoke
of a reformer lulling a society to change
of someone moonstruck sucking the sun's black tit

of a lake forgotten in the dark mirror
of flames furled like carrots in water
of things passed off well
of a conventional revolt
of a horizon in an orgasmic fog
there exists a domestic animal which likes to have a haircut.

Homage to G. V. Grunebaum

Here is my share of sand
A purple soul
Born in the desert
I was sheltered in a tent
They removed my foreskin
They showed me my totemic ancestor;
Picturesque vestiges without redemption
They taught me what is guts
What is ink
And granted me the Scripture
They let me thieve throughout the medieval nights
Holding the moon against the sun
Hitting on a solution
And when the day of Reason broke
They brought me a camel, the prophet's mount
And sent me to work amidst the debris
Splintering mirrors of otherness
In the hope of being attuned to that very rhetorisation
And before falling asleep
They advised me not to dream of perfection
It is lagging behind
They told me
Decay is in the present
Tomorrow is also decay
And everything will fall apart
Dust is master of all.

Hatif Janabi

Hatif Janabi was born in 1952 in Iraq. He has a BA in Arabic literature from Baghdad University. In 1976 he left for Poland, where he still lives, and where he gained an MA in Polish literature and a Ph.D. in drama. He has published eight volumes of poems, his latest in 1998, with five translated into Polish. He has also published works of criticism and literary translations into Arabic. He won the University of Arkansas Press Award for Arabic Literature in 1995. Selected poems were translated into English as *Questions and their Retinue* by Khaled Mattawa and published by the University of Arkansas Press. He is a member of Polish PEN.

The kingdom of dust

In the past, I used to toss words like stars
letting the sky harvest from them its wishes.
In the past I used to torture words:
a gazelle whinnied, a horse roared,
a frog sprinted, and pigeons brayed . . .
In the past, I was an old guard to an old gate,
a king to a kingdom of dust.
I was a blossom and a thorn,
a punctured blanket in the wind,
a needle moaning in a bed.
In the past, the past was a key and a lock.

What can I deny?
Can I deny the heart gashed with sins
and the tongue dusty with the dirt of words?
Can I deny the imam imploring me with rituals
and the gravedigger with his shovel,
and poetry as it whips me
with its chains and arrogance?
What can I do
in this wide wilderness?
In the past, I used to toss words like stars

letting the sky harvest from them its wishes.
In the past silence had
a sound and a meaning.

25 May 1997

You do not know

*Dedicated to my brother Mohammad, who died in the uprising in
southern Iraq at the end of the Gulf War, 1991*

> "What holy drink did you desire, my Lord,
> from this overflowing cup, this cup of my life?"
>
> *Tagore*

The day has narrowed and hope is mute.
My heart is on the wet grass,
and the evening keeps
its old shape.
The sidewalks
search for the victim's steps.
Their echo arrived from the south
anointed with grass and camphor,
and honeysuckle.

The Imam said: Have no fear, my son.
My body has been wrecked by steel and the cause.
"No" never equals "Yes".
Wails have deafened my ears.
You are my prodigal soul,
have no fear, my son.

Sadiq Street
was exalted with men's fear, crowded
with the turbulence of dust and frankincense.
The sidewalks sought refuge
under the haemorrhaging of blood
(woe to autumn
and its axe).

Space was
crowded.
Space has become
empty . . .

You do not know
how Turfa[1] gripped the unknown
in his own hands.
You know Hussain[2] by his rituals
and his severed head.
And the horizon by its blueness
and night by its stars
and love by its innocence.
You do not know
that night is winged,
thronged with gods, companions and maids,
and that glory is marked with a fugitive tear,
the beloved first shiver,
and the sorrows of hope . . .

You do not know
(Rimbaud)
or (Bajinski)[3] or (Sylvia).[4]
Sylvia –
you would have loved her
had you known her.
You do not know how this emptiness
is dreadful
how empty these tunnels are
and how impossible this dark.

You do not know
Face to face we huddle
by the bolted gate,
each clinging to his sins.

---

1 Turfa ibn al-Abd, a pre-Islamic poet, who unwittingly carried a letter to the King of
  Bahrain from the King of Hira ordering the former to kill the poet.

2 Imam Hussain, grandson of the Prophet Mohammad, murdered in Karbala.

3 Bajinski (1921–1944), an important Polish resistance poet who died in Warsaw.

4 Sylvia Plath (1932–1962).

In this grief-filled tunnel,
you plead.
Absence is your clothes
and your voice is the wind,
and your spirit
is the vast empty space.

You do not know
how impossible this darkness is.
You do not know.
You left too soon.

A wish

Hold my metal hand
and my towering shoulders.
Hold my seashell eyes
and my nose crooked like failure.
Hold my wooden fingers
and my forehead of mud
my teeth of reeds.
Hold my steps
        and my echo.
Hold my tongue that stretches
to the end of the horizon,
        and all that can make me a king
        a leader or a hero.

And leave me
my impetuousness,
and my childhood stutter.
Leave
my wild fancy
my free soul
my heart of gold.

12 January 1994

Translated by Khaled Mattawa

Nouri al-Jarrah

Nouri al-Jarrah was born in Damascus in 1956. Since 1981 he has lived in Beirut, Cyprus and London, working as a journalist, and interviewing many Arab literary figures. In London he established *al-Katiba* magazine. He has published six collections of his own poetry. He now lives in Cyprus and edits a new quarterly magazine, *al-Qaseeda*.

Elegy 1

To have gone back to Damascus
to have been able to.
To have left England,
to have opened a door in winter
and found all-glorious summer behind each opening.

Now . . . here . . . always . . .
England . . . with or without Damascus.
England, a grey time,
a shuddering of limbs,
and no escape
from the entanglement of leaf and thorn.
yet . . . Despair? Hope?
The day unbends.

To have gone back
and found Damascus . . .
something lacking,
completed,
was all mine.

Indifferent time topples thousands . . .
under weeping graves . . .
the assassinated and the assassin lie . . .

Judgement proceeds
with proud, respected gait,
the witness in his tattered clothes.
There goes the infant,
the orphaned life,
and the narrator . . . he . . . who encloses the sea
with his short story,
[writing what he sees];
often, he moved on further,
still writing what he saw.
Length and width, be probed the clamour,
then . . .
returning, he stretched and said:
I am the sleeping writer –
he seemed as dead as they were,
yet, he was fresh
as the flower in his hand.

To have found this door
To have found this hole of past eternity
and having found those simple pleasures . . .
a stroll . . . no more than the remnants of voices
    crushed by the crowd
engulfing the incoming rain.
The whisper of the past buttressed by the evening sky . . .
a whinnying horse moves across the frame . . .
fresh blood gushes from my shoulder . . .

Elegy 2

The denouement . . . but above and behind,
our retreat
saw in the last trail of summer
the spectre of a smile,
where flaked rocks whistled in danger,
pulled from under our feet with a curious sigh –
to fade . . . out of danger's reach.
The sun rose over the rocks

enflaming the shirt of the one who jumped in,
when you did,
triggering the rebound of youth
which would blossom among the thorns
parched the ponderous soul . . .
dry and heavy the land.

Scree slipping under your maladroit form,
the sun calls for you on the cliff,
taking the weight of the fall,
cushioning your knees.
Alas . . .
the breath of the thorns,
when they feebly break
weak or pale prayer.
I return to myself
as if it were yesterday.

Taken by a small stone,
as once I was moved to frequently,
holding it in my palm,
then letting it fall in the sun's sepulchre.

I dropped on my knees,
as if the air were oppressive,
the blood on my forehead odourless
. . . what aroma filled my lungs . . .
the pungence of the stunted tree.
The winds fell headlong
a wound stretching along the slope.

Only then,
I grasped the thing I once let go,
my smile at play with the thorns
its blurred trace torn, throbbing
in a giddy space.

Elegy 3

I desire light,
sleeplessness fills my eyes.
I am the remnant in a grave,
a wafted chrysalis –
though my form is dark and heavy.

I am not here, not there,
the rockface reverberates
silent interrogates . . .
lungs shattered . . .
all feeling lost,
the air, a drifting of torn leaves
almost inaudible.
I am the gust of wind
playing in a bright abyss.

Elegy 6

Her arm on the bed . . .
The open window bright on her arm,
colour undulates in light,
door and chair are witness
her sleep
a month long . . .
the room is radiant,
the glass silent
brings in new images . . .
with each breeze from the passage
uncertain shadows tremble.

No foot ever walked this paving,
no sound rises,
an eye, kohl half-applied
only death was bewildered and uncertain.
Death was forbidden here,

a chair blocked its way.
It stayed apart,
awaiting the tremble of light on her arm.

Elegy 7

Dear God, my lips are sealed,
my word an anchor.
From here . . . from the depths . . .
the outcry from one bed, my body elsewhere.

I am still spellbound,
haunting expired lives.
Dear God, I will surely remain
in the fissures of the day.
No light, no stalk even, or spike?
No blade to witness my smeared blood.
Dear God, every time,
always,
here,
sometimes.
The outspoken, the concealed.
Black waters flow, splitting my shoulders apart.

All that I'd imagined in sleeping . . . and waking.
the red rose,
black, as I mirrored it,
my hand burning,
I lift my gaze, the eyelid trembles.
Dear God, my poem burns white,
white as my hand.

Translated by Nawar al-Hassan Golley
with thanks to British poet David Kuhrt
and Patricia Kazan for valuable suggestions

Mohja Kahf

Mohja Kahf was born in Syria, and emigrated to the USA as a child. She has a Ph.D. in comparative literature from Rutgers University, and is assistant professor at Arkansas University, jointly in the English department and the Middle East Studies Program. Her poetry has been published in a number of magazines. She writes in English.

Men kill me

Men kill me
How they think the sun is all for them
and the water is all for them
How they accept the wind at their backs
as if the wind was the handmaid of their father
and they inherited her without a murmur

Men kill me,
how they think the earth of green and gold and God is all for
    them
How they feel generous in leaving one small spot
between four walls for all the women of the world
How they swallow all the meadows' wild colour upon
    colour
and feel grand if they remember to bring one red rose for a
    woman

Men kill me
How, if a woman takes one ray of the sun
or cuts a river through the water,
they accuse her of violating
the Copernican order
of upsetting the orbits of the planets
and the orbits of the pilgrims at the Ka'ba

Men kill me
How they forget that the world is resting

on the back of a tortoise
and the tortoise is poised on a spider
and the spider is dangling like a drop of sweat
from the temple of the woman scrubbing the floor
under the feet of Copernicus and the pilgrims at the Ka'ba

The road to Damascus

I am your translator
Don't you know that I was born
to translate you?

I am your translator
Don't you know
that no one else breathes your poetry
through both lungs –
who else has traded skin for scales,
become a fish and abandoned land,
just to glitter with the colours
of your sea?

I am your translator
and I am a woman of many powers,
queen of a magnificent throne:
Don't you know that only
the destined one can pull the sword
from the magic stone?

Don't you know
that I have been hoarding
a cache of ink for this
since time began?

Don't you know that I have been travelling
the road to this Damascus all my life,
waiting for this vision to overtake me?
I am your greatest convert –
Ah, how I shall bring the world
to kneel before your altar –

Of course I will betray you
All translators do
But it will be
a beautiful betrayal,
scattering stars,
cracking the earth,
defying the heavens,
slaying men and women –
a grand and terrible
and sweet betrayal –
infinitely
worthy of you

Canoe

His chest is the bark
of a canoe
in my capsized night
I find his nipples,
knots in the wood,
and he draws me in,
dripping,
to the dry hollow
of his heart

Ahmad Kattouah

Ahmed Kattouah was born in Jeddah in 1965. He graduated in political science from King Abdullah Aziz University in 1988, and presented arts programmes for Saudi Arabian radio from 1985 to 1991. Since 1984 he has published his poems in several literary and arts magazines in Saudi Arabia and the Arab world, and has one published collection to his name. He currently works in the Saudi Arabian diplomatic service.

Surprise

Peacefully
the road sips its coffee
shoes chatter
sidewalks listen
suddenly
from neighbouring windows
a lamp flees
like a wonderful
old thief
who from afar
has been watching his barefoot shadow
and contemplating flight.

Dissolution

His head feels light
he lets it
flutter away

Transience

A sunrise like this
what to do with that orange on the horizon?
Quarter it, send sections to far-away friends?
Or drizzle its juice onto the dirt
so you can etch in the foam
a prelude to transience?

Isolation

The foreigner
whose face is stormy with sorrow beneath
the city's bright ceiling, who swallows hardship
with his daily bread,
leans against his preoccupations and gazes
into the distance, seeking warmth in the shelter
of his isolation.

Attempt

All right then
if brightness is a wall before you
why not splatter it
with your gloom?

Claws

His pet pains
the ones he raised for his old age
drip down the sides of his head like honey
race ahead of him on the stairs to open the door . . .

Today
they stained their claws
with the red of his heart.

Visit

Eyes drowsy
and slightly red,
the semi-darkness like thick glass
do not straighten your posture
allow your trunk to stiffen thus
perhaps tonight a woodcutter
will visit you.

Evidence

How luxurious
and laced with an opulent sweetness
to sever a rose's limb
and pluck its feathers with two fingers
but you, too, are impure
bent like a nail
against a wall.

The rose and the nail
what links them
besides a thread of blood
leading to you?

Translated by Seema Atalla

Waleed Khazendar

Waleed Khazendar was born in 1950 in Gaza. He has published three collections of poetry. In October 1997 he was awarded the Palestine Prize for Poetry for "his achievements and aesthetic originality in the prose poem". During 1998–1999 he was Arab Writer in Residence at the Near East Studies Programme, Oxford University. He now lives and works in Cairo.

The same perfume

She wasn't behind a handwave,
and not because a rustling touched me.
I went down the stairs rising
from the baggage gallery, and didn't find her.
And at the bus station I didn't find her
a short foolish woman
with a small wound near her navel.

She didn't come.
And I won't know how much she's changed.

Does she still, like last year, bang the wall
with her head whenever she rages,
and still take off to the end of the earth
because of a word I say.
Does she still put on the perfume I don't like
and wear the colours I hate
and leave her things scattered about
here and there, on the ropes of my nerves?
Is she still the day's obstinate boy?
The high waves of night?
When I opened the door
her suitcases didn't surprise me.
Her mad scattered things now, here, did not surprise me,

not even the water splattering in the bath,
not even her singing.

I was following, from the garden door,
the same perfume
her perfume that I don't like.

A needle and angels

Not only this evening
but usually, about this time, the trees slacken:
when we come closer to the waves
and the lights are lost in darkness
and the sun becomes a red island at the end of the sea.

It is not only when you reach a hand to me
and adjust – at about this time – my collar,
that I remember I am distracted and distant
and that I still keep the lights on
afraid of my grandmother's ghoul,
but also when I stray in your hands
as you line demons on my pillow
and mend my buttons
with thread and needle and angels.

Night is a flash

He doesn't know where
this door leads
nor why the plants around him
are yellowed and drooping.
What confuses him most
are the roses
thirsty, silent, nonchalant
intimately clutching their colours.

The horses on the wall
are tired and grey
almost blackened by the clouds.

Why is he here now?
Doesn't he have, other than here, friendships
dawn, fantasies, and a coffee pot.

And isn't the wolf closer to his nature?
Hasn't he himself said:
        the horizon a needle
        a thicket of foxthorns then!

One moment, he doesn't know how, out there
his face resembles him again.
The air is a magician and the shadows are tokens.
The trees are busy
with their fruit, and night is a flash.

Half the night

His touch is wheat
when with tired hands he taps on our shoulders,
and a cypress rises in his silence
because he does not complain.

We did not understand grains then.
We did not understand dew.
He used to share a loaf of bread, like a miracle, among us
and share his days and commandments.

Keep it, always, hot
your bread, after me.

Past midnight, he wanders,
his tobacco between his fingers,
peering through our rooms
counting us
covering whatever we've left exposed

looking out from the window
distant and ponderous.

My mother, who is
a thousand and one labyrinths,
all morning
follows his ember
ash by ash.

A short while, a city

Here, they will settle, a short while, a city:
They were tired, their herds too,
and the wheat in their sacks shivered.

They will wound time here
with houses, like their imaginations
haphazard, stranded
straying room by room
from the bow of their lives into infinity.

Below sea-level
they will mould urns from clay,
dazed, delicate and more perfect.
Slowly, they will lift
their heads to the sun
and quietly look down.
They are listening to the softness of copper
between two rivers in its shaping.
They hear it ringing
cry by cry, in eternity.

Distant light

Harsh and cold
autumn holds to it our naked trees:

If only you would free, at least, the sparrows
from the tips of your fingers
and release a smile, a small smile
from the imprisoned cry I see.

Sing! Can we sing
as if we were light, hand in hand
sheltered in shade, under a strong sun?
Will you remain, this way
stoking the fire, more beautiful than necessary, and quiet?

Darkness intensifies
and the distant light is our only consolation –
that one, which from the beginning
has, little by little, been flickering
and is now about to go out.

Come to me. Closer and closer.
I don't want to know my hand from yours.
And let's beware of sleep, lest the snow smother us.

Rod of commandments

Our mistakes, out of our hands,
precede us, always, to the pillow.
They remain between an eyelid and another,
an hour, or so long as they wish.
They wave at us the rod of commandments.
They take us to the ghoul's room
to the black hyena
to the scorpion's cave.

Our small mistakes
our spoiled mistakes
always rise before us.
They shower
and comb their hair
and watch themselves a long while

in our mirrors,
and they may grow
before we wake, and become beautiful.

A chair for the suitcase

The one missing at five
the one missing from the dim corner
of the station café
a blue metallic circle
a chair for him
a chair for the suitcase
a chair to gaze at
long and absentmindedly.

And while he does not drink the coffee
does not listen to the people, trains, or songs
while, like an ancient statue
he neither begins nor ends,
he says nothing and never leaves the story.

By then the five-thirty train had left.

Translated by Khaled Mattawa

Vénus Khoury-Ghata

Vénus Khoury-Ghata was born in 1937, in Besherri, the village of Gibran Kahlil Gibran in Lebanon. She studied literature, and began publishing her poetry in 1969. She has published 14 novels and 13 collections of poems. In 1980 she won the Apollinaire Prize for Poetry, followed by the Mallarmé Prize in 1987, the Grand Prix of the French Society of Authors in 1990, and the Prix Supervielle in 1998. Her highly acclaimed autobiographical novel, *La maison au bord des larmes* (Editions Balland) was published in 1999. She lives in Paris.

The seven honeysuckle-sprigs of wisdom

My village has three waterfalls three churches but no priest
The last one went off after a crow that cawed in Aramaic

Time in my village is so rushed that women conceive and
    bear children in seven days no skimpier than the ones
    you'd see elsewhere

My village's river turns back towards its source to avoid
    flowing through the neigbouring hamlet with its wealth of
    three cars and an embalmed saint which attracts pilgrims

Mordechai the hairdresser has painted a devil on his door to
    ward off thieves
His left hand cuts hair in secret on the Sabbath
the knife gripped between his jaws
It's to cut into the bread of sorrow while still curling the
    rabbi's hair

Mordechai is neither believer nor heretic but balsamic like
    the vinegar in which Rachel's duck simmers when she has
    her period

Rachel never closes her door for fear of wearing out the
    hinges and keeping happiness from entering her house

The milkman who's mad about her says that she's so hairy
that his donkey could graze in her armpits while he shot
off his rifle and chewed on lupine grass

Philomena's thoughts are as narrow as her skirts her soul as
high as her heels which are mired in timidity since she
started knitting a vest for the paint-merchant

Amine is so wealthy that seven different-coloured salts stand
in state on his table
The rainbow which has a place at his table plunges its
fingers seven times in a row in his jars before making a
brief appearance on his balcony to the applause of passers-
by

It happened that Jacob saw horses galloping on the roof of
the synagogue with the moon which mocked them in
crude words from the Kabbala
"Thank God it's only a dream" he stammered as he fell back
to sleep
Jacob's daughter, who had the misfortune of dreaming the
same dream, was turned into a casserole
spices and smoke were stirred together into her eyes

Laouza goes into town every month to have her back
photographed
Pain is cutting her in two ever since she fell from the cherry
tree which grew more quickly than her ladder
Her ewe's milk has turned black since a lizard gave her the
evil eye through the skylight

This selfsame Laouza's pot of gardenias doesn't cheer up her
parakeets which come from India and which only smile at
the postman who should bring them news from their
cousins in New Delhi

The miser Mantouf divides his chestnuts between his pigs
and the Armenian saint beatified for political reasons
The latter swallows them without pleasure and then excretes
them in the holy-water front wrapped in paper from
Armenia

Mantouf was a schoolmaster before he inadvertently
   straddled a toad
A wellspring of science and information
he spat knowledge right into the children's mouths
and paid the butcher with buttons he tore off his fly

Mantouf's wife has ears as tender as vine-leaves beneath the
   arbour
a neck as supple as a syringa leaf in the sun
A bottle of vinegar shares her bed since her husband has
   been sleeping with the rivulet
He comes home at dawn
his two fists clenched on his chest turned into pebbles

The legs of this selfsame Mantouf have grown shorter since
   his wife washed his pants
With the extra fabric, she made three vests, a pair of trousers
   and a bow-tie for the parish beggar

The priest, the rabbi and the imam, invited to the poor man's
   table,
brought him three tufts of their beards which he planted in
   his garden
The three upside-down trees which grew three months later
cast their shade on the devil's house

The schoolmaster Farhoud is so conscientious that he tries
   the alphabet out on himself before using on the children
The letter Aleph is unreliable
its back is so fragile even a hair couldn't ride on it
"Mim" is an ardent she-camel listening to the muezzin
"Ba" prefers jam to the dictionary
"Zah's" axles creak since "tah" crushed its toe
"Tah" can only be learned lying down while standing up
   he's a nasty one
Farhoud lived in geography for a long time before moving
   into grammar
Asia Minor he says is only Asia Major's younger sister
and the poles an invention of a bear with a bad idea

Farhoud can argue both sides of every question
in favour of the beggar on the square, promising him that
   after he dies he'll eat partridges at every meal
against his neighbour, saying that other people's bread
   doesn't fill your belly

Farhoud had a wife before he had a book
whom he leafed through every morning in the direction the
   sheets went
from left to right as one speaks French
in the direction of the windmills of Holland

Farhoud adopted three orphans with one month's salary
three racoons who foraged on garbage cans in Montreal

Monsier Antoun sleeps in his tarboosh to show his scorn of
   the French colonists
From far off, you'd take him for a poppy with just one petal
He earned the medals which cluster on his pyjama jacket
he emerged victorious from a battle with a whole hive of
   bees after he rubbed the drone's nose

Antoun's wife isn't the same since a pidgeon shat on her
   head
she makes eyes at the stained-glass saint
and asks the stream for a light for her cigarette

Antoun's sister Khaoula has marmoreal thighs
volcanic breasts
and the crotch of a sergeant with hair as straight as
   matchsticks

Translated from the French by Marilyn Hacker

Adel Khuzam

Adel Khuzam is a Saudi poet, born in Bahrain in 1963. He has lived all his life in the United Arab Emirates. He has a degree in accountancy and management from the University of the Emirates. Since 1982 he has regularly contributed his poetry, and articles on the arts, to newspapers and literary magazines in the Middle East. He published his first collection of poetry in 1993 and the second in 1997. He is an accomplished musician, and works as a journalist on *al-Khaleej* newspaper in Sharjah.

Standing between a tall woman's thighs during war

The opposites were rubbed together.
A spark flew over the grass
another over the water.
Head to head the opposites were rubbed
causing a lot of skulls to break.
The old meaning was massacred.
The disaster ended peacefully.

Today the swans
return undisturbed to their lakes.
The insect goes back to the rubbish dump,
man to his house in the wilderness.
Today, when one dog
is not much of a guard
and standing between a tall woman's thighs
is not enough either.

Getting out

The wall grows silent
forever, creatures scatter about

enviable in their designations,
and you fall prey to symbols.
Get out. Rise.
No one, besides you, is waiting.
One leap against this silence,
The end is hidden under your shoe.
The road belongs to the barefoot,
The fugitives and martyrs,
The road that twists
like a rope around the neck.

The well

The wise man said:
the well is the opposite
of your secret; how easy
to look into, and terrible
to fall to its bottom.
There the mighty lion
once fell to his death.
The giraffe stretched his neck
through its throat
and was turned into an inverted
Eiffel Tower.

He said this
as if to describe
my own feelings of suffocation.

Translated by Sargon Boulus

Wafa'a Lamrani

Wafa'a Lamrani was born in 1960 in al-Qasr al-Kabir, Morocco. In 1982 she received her diploma in Arabic literature from the College of Literature and Humanities in Rabat. She lectures in Mohammedia and lives in Casablanca. She is general secretary of the House of Poetry in Morocco. Lamrani has published three collections, and read her work at many Arab and European poetry festivals.

The eighth day

> "And he said to me: the day of death is the wedding day
> and the day of solitude is the day of cheerfulness."
> *al-Niffari*

1 Root

I was born of a sentiment that resembles neither love nor
    hatred; it often resembles pride.
They did not want me, but I came. By force I emerged the
    moment I desired.
Before the beginning I identified with defiance
I announced that I, together with the age, were split on the
    edge of alienage,
That I, together with time, were forever two times. . .

2 Genesis

From insight I initiate
My genesis
I extend along a space narrower than the eye of the needle,
I feign permeation into my own substance.
The wind of the hollow comes from neither al-Sham nor al-
    Maghreb.*

---

* Al-Sham – Syria and the northern Middle East. Al-Maghreb – Morocco and North Africa.

Thus do I depart:
Departure could not carry me away,
Nor could transit escape me,
Nor even could arrival entomb me.

3 Body

Whenever the voice of the body waxes ecstatic
The femininity of wisdom blossoms
And with roses covers those of its own parts
That remain dreamy in their coyness.
I saddle the footsteps for craving . . .

4 Love

My free tender heart
I have posted on the highest summit of the Atlas Mountains,
For the stinking hyenas
Are accustomed to decadence
And heights usually make them feel
Dizzy and nauseous . . .
My heart is a flower mined with fragrance
But the picker is a chronic common cold!

5 Semiotica

I emerge out of the blast of a time
That comes not,
I tame the leakage of seconds,
I spill them as signatures of a lifetime
Crammed with departures . . .

6 Bleeding

The loneliness of the evenings consumes me,

It nibbles at my passion
And then casts me off as a fragment
For the fugitive glow.

7 Pattern

If there were a meaning
If there were a colour
If there were a day
Not the Monday mail
Not the Tuesday train
Not the Wednesday laundry
Not the Thursday meeting
Not the Friday nausea
Not the Saturday loneliness
Not the Sunday ennui.
Oh, how weary is the Sunday afternoon . . .
If there were a face instead of a face,
A figure instead of a figure,
A lifetime instead of this lifetime,
A time instead of this time,
A sun instead of the sun,
An earth instead of the earth,
If there were an air that is really like air . . .
I am weary of what's around me, weary of parts of me,
     weary of my entire self.
I am weary of being a muse for poets, weary of the earth that
     is not up to me, weary of the sky.
I am weary of my colleague, who backbites me, and of the
     street that molests me,
of my brother who bothers me and never cares for me.
I am weary of my dwelling and of my time.
I am weary of weariness and of myself,
I deny all conditions and am weary even of denial.
If there were a day,
A colour,
A meaning . . .

8 Coronet

What does the wisdom of the body say?
"Forlornness is pleasanter than weariness,
Gentler than rock."
This is why the eighth day is mine:
So that the letter may on that day impregnate me
And I give birth to twins
So that death may on that day utter me
And thus I get cured . . .

23 February 1992

Translated by Hassan Hilmy

Fatima Mahmoud

Fatima Mahmoud was born in Libya. She worked as a journalist from 1976 to 1987, and in 1984 published her first collection of poems. Eventually she left Libya for Cyprus, where she co-founded and edited *Modern Sheharazade* magazine. In 1995 she sought political asylum in Germany.

Wounds that resemble me

I want
to hang this trampled
evening
on the kerosene cart on its way
to a calm-nerved
explosion.
This evening
in the shape of a geriatric afternoon.
I want to hang
this evening
in a poster, and go on . . .
the soul of a renegade slave
loafing about
the galaxy
   leaving/
   this sand
   these cities
   this tedium . . . for another Job
   to emerge from the horror of myths

I want
to hang this evening
on
the tiles of a closed window
and pass/
   tucked

in the rolled sleeve of an iris/
calling
for the the morning to emerge
from the sheath
of the previous night . . .
A child
scrubs a white surprise
from his eyes
He opens windows
onto colourful
cities,
and launches a savage celebration.
I want
to attend
his festival
to bar the poets from
pruning
this surprise

I want to
hang this
evening
on the balcony and pass on
scissors and pads/
I tear this
closed horizon/
and the blood of its pride
spills in a black
haemorrhage.
I want to
dress
wounds
that resemble me.

I want
to hang this evening
onto another evening
and pass on –
a sword of cellophane
to prick the throats

of the sulphurous vapours
rising from contorted buildings . . .
A false confession
is broadcast from the offices of neon
into the grinding gears of the soul.
I want to climb
the staircase of confession
to God in his forced
confinement
in the divine garb.
     I say
      this screaming,
      this falsification
      this well-made alibi
      do not
      resemble us.
What resembles us
  is your freedom

I want
to hang this evening
on questions
      and pass on . . .
      More wings
      more light
      more
      freedom
      more
      more
        of myself

Translated by Khaled Mattawa

Salman Masalha

Salman Masalha was born in 1953 in al-Maghar, Galilee. He has a
Ph.D. in Arabic literature from the Hebrew University of Jerusalem
where he now lives and teaches Arabic language and literature. He
is co-editor of a series publication, *Early Arabic Poets*. He has published
four collections of his own poetry, as well as articles and literary
translations in newspapers and journals, in both Arabic and Hebrew,
including his Hebrew translation of Mahmoud Darwish's *Memory
for Forgetfulness*. His own poems have themselves been translated
into several languages and published in various anthologies and
magazines.

On deserts

When I wander, in search of pasture,
as was ordained for me in my ancient books,
I take along some blank sheets of paper,
and a fax machine. Sometimes I also embrace
a Walkman, tuned only to
FM stations. I have no need
for medium, nor short waves, for aerials
are useless in the deserts of Rub' al-Khali,
as they are with my scattered tribe, especially
on my mother's side. And I'm afraid that
in the heat of my self-search and the chill
of catching my tattered breath,
gales and sandstorms pick
me up. Instead, I revel
in thirsty echoes, flowed back
with the sun, carrying memories
of an old tune, gathered by the wind
from far and near. And when
I'm startled from my afternoon nap,
I look at my naked body,
and wonder how they stuck to it,
the females of sand. I pull them off

my body, like a hair from my soul's dough.
And thus, with my herds and hard rifts,
I move around my ancient wilderness
until the end of time,
and no one sees me.

Wireless

1

Some sips away from the steaming
coffee, from the cigarettes that smoke
out the clouds – the colours rest
on the mall's sidewalks.
Birds send out their wireless
messages. I'm all ears,
listening carefully, hunting down
the migrant tips.

2

In the city of my anonymity,
I fear the most exposing
lovers: they flock in
from Ramallah and Bethlehem,
celebrating their secrets
in the unfamiliar streets.

3

The wild clouds are oblivious
to city folks. The lovers here
failed to tame them: there they pass,
not asking for permission, dropping
their loads upon their heads.
Then dash off to hide behind
the upper floors. But hide and seek
doesn't play well in the holy city.
For God sees everything.
And so do I.

The partridge tail

1
A deserted homeland on my lips.
Shaking off its shoulders
grains of wheat
that were caught up in the hair.

2
Among the olive groves
the peasant draws memory's furrows
and forgets all about the birds of the wilderness
coveting his seeds.

3
Upon the stone palms
the morning clouds are dripping,
pressed by the hills
from all sides.

4
The hunter fills his bag with rags
and sticks a partridge tail on top
for people to acknowledge
his hunting skills.

Translated by Anton Shammas

Maram al-Massri

Maram al-Massri was born in 1962 in Latakia in Syria. She studied English literature at Damascus University, and started publishing her poetry in Arab magazines in the mid-1970s. Her second collection won the Adonis Prize for Poetry in 1998. Some of her poems have been translated into French and Spanish. She lives in Paris.

2

How foolish:
Whenever my heart
hears a knocking,
it opens its doors.

3

Desire preoccupies me
and my eyes shine.
I stuff morals
in the nearest drawer.
I switch into a devil
and blindfold my angels
just
for a kiss

14

Women like me
do not know how to speak.
A word remains in their throats
like a thorn
they choose to swallow.
Women like me
know nothing but weeping,

impossible weeping
suddenly
pumping
like a severed artery.
Women like me
receive blows
and do not dare return them.
They shake with anger;
they subdue it.
Like a lion in a cage
women like me
dream . . .
of freedom . . .

20

I killed my father
that night
or the other day –
I don't remember.
I go escaping with a suitcase
filled with dreams
and amnesia,
and a picture of me
with him
when I was young
and when he carried me
on his forearm.

I buried my father
in a beautiful shell
in a deep ocean,
but he found me
hiding under the bed
shaking with fear
and loneliness

40

He wanted
no more than this:
a house, children
and a wife
who loved him.
But he woke up one day
and found that his spirit
had grown old.

She wants
not more than this:
a house and children
and a husband who loves her.
She woke up
one day
and found
that her spirit
had opened a window
and fled.

52

He came to me
disguised in the body of a man
and I paid him no attention.
He told me
"Open up.
I am the holy ghost."
I feared to disobey him
and I let him kiss me.
He uncovered
my shy breasts
with his gaze
and turned me into
a beautiful woman.
Then he blew his spirit
into my body,

rumbling
thunder and lightning.
And I believed.

57

You should not
have touched my hand
and left it dreaming
of your touch.

You should not
have kissed my lips
and left them burning
for your crush.

You should have
remained quiet
so that I would not stop
hoping.

103

Like grains of salt
they shone
then melted.
This is how they disappeared
those men
who did not love me.

Translated by Khaled Mattawa

Khaled Mattawa

Khaled Mattawa was born in Libya in 1964 and emigrated to the USA when he was 15. From 1995-1996 he was Alfred Hodder Fellow at Princeton University. In 1998 he became the first Arab-American to win a Guggenheim Poetry Fellowship. He has won various awards for his writing and is widely anthologised as part of a new wave of American poets. In 1995, his first poetry collection *Ismailia Eclipse* was published by Sheep Meadow Press, USA. He has translated many Arab poets into English, published two books of modern Arab poetry in translation, and co-edited *Post Gibran: Anthology of New Arab American Writing*. He has taught creative writing in several universities in the USA and has recently joined the English faculty at the University of Texas, Austin. He writes in English.

River psalms

Mountains were born to steal
snow from the stars.
Then the seas were parched
and mountains sent riverly messages
sang riverly psalms.
A river reaches the sea
and lays a wet kiss on its cheeks.
It opens miles of embrace. It whispers:
      you must never leave me;
      you must not drown the hills

There are no rivers where I live.
The mountains are sheered sheep
exhausted by hot sun.
When snow falls, the sands suck it
and leave us red mud fields.
We draw rivers with our fingers
and build straw ships and feather sails.
When the valleys flood, we tear down
the neighbours' fences and sing:

let the river go
let the waters flow

The Nile is a preacher
who crosses the desert alone.
He walks a straight path
to a paradise of reeds.
At dawn he builds a city
for the sun to rise in;
at dusk he razes fields
for the sun to bed.
He is the moon's tired lover,
worksongs nesting in his head

Torn trousers, limbs frosted
with shiny mud, the Amazon
is a fat drunk lost in woods.
When he wanders too far
the sea pounds on his chest
and fish bite at his sleeves.
The stars gleam their consolations,
and the monkeys wail:
      why us   why now
      too soon   too soon

My rivers were a star fish
and God's counting hand.
I calmed dust so it would not spread
thin films on storeroom shelves,
so it would not print blood-
shot eyes on cabbage leaves.
And I sent my city's brackish water
to every levy to every ravine.
And on and on I whispered:
      Mississippi, Yang Tzi
      O my Niger, O Mekong

Visiting Jonah

I dip my feet in water,
see black ships,
multi-colored flags.
But this water is salty
and that's what keeps ships afloat.
Pardon me.
Lately I have been borrowing
other people's wishes. Pardon
my wish to die in sunshine.
I am bewitched
by what my hands can do.
In my mail I receive packages
for the heartless.
A helicopter brings me
livers on ice.
Lungs in saline solution
come in the afternoon.
I can cut you up
and change your parts,
sew you together,
tuck you in to sleep. Sometimes,
I lose my hands and my arms shiver.
Sometimes, I wrestle with Jacob
and he tosses my feet to the dogs.
Moses strikes me with his stick.
His followers laugh until
their golden dentures slip.
I visit Jonah
in his room of flesh.
"The world is not much
bigger than this whale,"
he tells me as we sit
in darkness breathing air
heavy with blood and salt.

Hunger

for Joe Bolton

How this hunger comes
I may never know – the hollowness
in bones, brittling of hair,
thinning of skin are but symptoms.
Where do you take such pain?
Where can you cash it in?
Where do fingers travel
after they lose their touch?
I am caught up in the boom
of abandonment, in the glimmer,
the shining of conceit.
The baby found alive in a dumpster
last week is no relative
to the one that got crushed today.
And my father's heart, the walls
of which are becoming thinner
with every pint of blood,
is no relative to mine which
longs for a whiff of the breeze
of freshly baked loaves.

What my hands tell you is a noise
my heart is deaf to. The ground
under me will sprout with seaweed,
wild artichoke, and prickly pear.
You can reach for an imaginary thorn
and a drop will flow from your fingertips.
You can lick them and heal, but only after
a thousand moons have passed.
Your self-pity will take you places;
sympathy cards will drown you
in their tears. Go, go
join the one-legged men
who trod the earth leaving
left-footed tracks, who believe

the earth is a pyramid. To the top
they will climb at an appointed hour,
on a day the smoke of burning lilies
suffocates an asthmatic moon.

Ubbad

1968 – Nasser – Sinai gone –
& every time I say repentance
enthusiasm enraptures
floors & beams to creaking – sweat
tears & soda (Soviet made)
pour on melancholy's grimy floors
I'm tossed by the strong
arms of fate – his liver –
only he can feel the flame
burn of flesh & I miss
his black eyes & longing
melts me away – Congas
rondel a theft from
the honorable steadfast
people of Cuba and Cougat –
so the horn section maligns
the green heart like mad
potter hands thumbing
smoke thick air – Did I say
the songs are wilting
in cotton fields – Suror
on tenor sax pawning
fellahin tunes & Taha
fluting the Pharoah's chant
& every time I say repentance
crowds howl – a song seeded
years ago – an adobe hut
in Minya & a swaddled baby
cursing the almighty's good
for nothing name

Taproot and cradle

They aired their complaints
until the last bird flew,
and a song wafted, a song about long ago.
Fists balled in my pocket,
I carry the wish and the wound.

Who calls my name from the window now?
Evening coffee, and my mother salts her evening broth –
not the quantity, but the flick of her wrist -
and my mother bakes bread,
and my mother hobbles, her knees locked,
and my mother carries
the soft stones of her years.

It's raining in a noisy town,
the inhabitants' cruel happy words,
their sighs, and laughs that slide
from their bellies like small marsupials.
And the city trudges, and the night trudges,
a stolen bulldozer,
a tank full of clowns.

She touches her hair now.
(Who is she that I am remembering now?)
She caresses her beauty like the coffin of a child.
The ocean.
Shadows on the square.

My pen of late arrivals.
My knife of darkened temples.
My words scurrying, my frantic mice,
My drunken snakes . . .
I am caressing cool hands with rain.
I am remembering the killed enemy,
remembering my good friends.

Bassem al-Mereiby

Bassem al-Mereiby was born in Iraq in 1960 and studied acting and theatre direction in Baghdad. He has published four collections of poems and his first, *al-'Atil 'An al-Wardah*, published in 1988 in London, won the Youssef al-Khal Prize for Poetry. He lives now in Sweden.

A land woven by pirates

In the land made of the gaze
a hawk fixes on his prey
there are words that constantly echo
words that endlessly spin
between two birds on a solitary tree
between the sacrifice and its horror
between stream and stone
between shadow and fire.

Terror-stricken land
is what remains of a dead man's gaze
the whisper of a splintered tree
at the doorstep of an axe dipped in sparks
sparks that can light up the blackness of roots.
In the book of darkness
where the gloom glistens
with the fate of the trees
and the axe
and the river
full of pre-dawn stars
night shines more brightly
and secrets are doubly hushed.

In places that shun words
and lie in ferocity and blood
and in promises and tears

I look at people –
how they are served their misery to drink
and how they are turned into firewood
in the forests of their ruin.

In the land ransomed with a tear
there are only happy pirates
following an imaginary river
to a stillborn treasure.

Lands that pile up
in the fabulous maps of skilled pirates
and lands that pour
through forgotten rivers
and falling rocks
and feet falling from cliffs
through maps stolen from bloodlines.
One land remains
a suspended tear
between the eye
and the scene it views.

My father

Perhaps my father
is the scent of evening sprinkled on villages
and the fragrance of a dawn dripping with calm
washed with rooster crows
and the sound of the distant coughing of a labourer in mud
and the waking of women to morning ovens
and the return of greenery to far-away views.
Perhaps my father is the blood-letting of night with songs
and the smoke rising from guest houses
and the flow of the Euphrates through the weeping of
    viaducts.

And my father . . .
the trembling song knocking on the princess's door

And my father . . . a minaret
   lifting the heart with a chant of yearning
and my father a restive cup
   and a dreamy hand sobbing with mud
and my father, from excess of longing,
   chains the soul to the depths of the Euphrates
   and sings to the land of sugarcane
and my father
   a flintstone tied to a belt of fatigue

Blind ink

Blind ink
and idle letters

is all that remains
between us.

Mail

Since the time of ancient wounds
night has surrendered us to morning
and morning has passed up on to mail

Translated by Khaled Mattawa

Dunya Mikhail

Dunya Mikhail was born in Baghdad in 1965. She studied English literature at Baghdad University and has published three collections of poetry. She has lived in Michigan, USA, since 1996 and is studying for an MA degree in oriental studies at Wayne State University.

The war works hard

The war
How serious
  and active
    and skilful
        It is!

From early morning
It wakes up the sirens
  sends ambulances everywhere
  swings corpses in the air
  slides stretchers to the wounded
  summons rain from the eyes of mothers
  digs in the earth
  shovels many things from under the ruins
some lifeless glittering things
others pale and still throbbing

It brings more inquiries
to the minds of children
entertains the gods
by shooting missiles and fireballs
through the sky

It plants mines in the fields
  harvests holes and air-pockets
  urges families to emigrate
  stands with the clergymen

as they curse the devil
(The wretched one, his hand is still in the fire. It hurts)

The war is relentless, day and night.
It inspires tyrants to deliver long speeches
   gives medals to generals
and themes to poets

It contributes to the industry of artificial limbs
   provides food for flies
   adds pages to the book of history
   achieves equality between victim and murderer
   teaches lovers to write letters
   trains girls to wait
   fills newspapers with stories and photos
   beats drums to celebrate every year
   builds new houses for the orphans
      keeps coffin-makers very busy
   pats the shoulders of gravediggers
   draws a smile on the leader's face.

The war works very hard
without precedent
yet nobody praises it.

Pronouns

He plays a train
She plays a whistle
They move away

He plays a rope
She plays a tree
They swing

He plays a dream
She plays a feather
They fly

He plays a General
She plays people
They declare war.

The Cup

The woman turned the cup upside down
Amid the figures and letters
She turned the light off and
Only one candle remained burning
She put her finger on the cup
And repeated some words:
"You, spirit, if you attend, say yes"
The cup moved to the right
The woman said: Are you the spirit
of my husband, the martyr?
The cup moved to the right – YES
She said: Why did you leave me that soon?
The cup moved to the letters
I COULD NOT HELP IT
She said: Why did you not escape?
The cup moved ⟶ I DID
She said: How were you killed, then?
The cup moved ⟶ FROM BEHIND
She said: What will I do now with all this loneliness?
The cup did not move
She said: Do you love me?
The cup moved to the right for YES
She said: Can I keep you here?
The cup moved to the left for NO
She said: Can I come with you?
The cup moved ⟶ NO
She said: Will our life change?
The cup moved to the right
She said: When?
The cup moved ⟶ 1996
She said: Are you OK?
The cup moved slowly to the right

She said: What do you advise me?
The cup moved ⟶ ESCAPE
She said: To where?
The cup did not move
She said: Will we know more catastrophes?
The cup did not move
She said: What is your will?
The cup moved to a meaningless sentence
She said: Are you tired of my questions?
The cup moved to the left
She said: Can I ask more?
The woman said, after some silence:
"You, spirit, go in peace"
She turned the cup upright
and blew out the candle.
Then she called out to her son
who was catching insects in the garden
in a helmet full of holes.

Translated by the author

Zakaria Mohammed

Zakaria Mohammed was born in 1951 in Janin, Palestine. He studied Arabic literature at Baghdad University. He has published two collections of poetry and a novel (1997), and in 1999 he published a collection of plays. He now lives in Ramallah, Palestine, and is deputy editor of Mahmoud Darwish's *al-Karmel* magazine.

Coming home

I left and came back

What was green had ripened

Fodder for caterpillars
Flesh to be chewed on like qat

The rose and the bull

At night the rose is dark

At night a black bull
flies from the rose
It pierces the skin
with its two silver horns

At night the rose is dark
The spilt blood
of the hapless passer-by
drips from its horns

At night the rose is dark

But in daylight
the rose's black bull

is only a shadow
lying in ambush

So beware
when you pick
the rose
Beware

Carry a dagger
close to your heart
to butcher
that bull

which lies
all day
folded in petals
at the heart of the rose

Night

Night is opening its poisonous flower
It seeps through the sky
like a tincture spilt into water

Night is unfurling its flower
for the solitary insomniacs
who stumble along from step to step

Night is enfolding the city
as the homeless come out
from their doorways and basements

Night is opening its poisonous flower
as dread rolls down the stairs
like a melon

The last one

Spare me
the last bullet in the revolver
so death can wait at the doorway

Spare me
the last gasp in the lungs
so breath can expire with hard labour

Spare me
the last copy of the key
so only the ghosts can get in

My crazy sister

The daffodil bulbs are tucked safe underground
The wind is teasing the grasses

I warn my mad sister:
Don't bother the daffodils
Don't poke at the earth with your fingers

Then wind blew right through me
and the fig tree was bare

We went inside and turned up the oil lamp
ate last year's potatoes for supper

At midnight my sister slipped from her bed
All night she tore at the earth with bare hands

craving the light of the daffodil bulbs

The jug

Smash it with your stick,
my love

this fragile jug,
my heart

Splash its liquid
in the dust

or hold it high
above your head

to let it spill
into your mouth

But don't touch your lips
with its ochre clay:

Death is fired
on the lip of the jug

death is fired
in its clay

The journey

It happens you wander into the wilderness
You lose your sense of direction

You ascend the steep hills
You descend into valleys

Your boots get stuck in the mud
Walking's exhausting, so you rest for a while

then find you're too knackered to move
I'll camp here for the night, you decide

Then you spot a donkey
so grey it looks hewn out of limestone

Grazing methodically
it doesn't jump when you mount it

but seems happy to take you
back to a path that looks very familiar

The donkey trots on patiently
knowing each bend and curve of the road

You settle into the rhythm
feeling secure now

watching the landscape pass by
watching the sun set in an out-of-sight ocean

You are on your journey
You are taking the road

So what if you don't know the way?
The donkey knows the way

and the donkey is death

The heart

is a paper eagle
        coasting over
an arboretum of wind

Untitled

Father, what are these trees
that stretch to the horizon
in an unbroken row?

The dead, my son,
who left for the war
and couldn't return

Watch them line up
like peasants at checkpoints
longing to enter the city

But the huge gates are barred
and the watchtowers are manned
with fire and with arrows all night

The second brother

I followed in your footsteps
I trod in your shadow

till you fell
in the pit of the dead

They made me first
the ram with no horns

But I will be second forever
forever printing my footprints

over those invisible footprints
that stretch out into pitch dark

Translated by Sarah Maguire
in collaboration with the author

Adnan Mohsen

Adnan Mohsen was born in Baghdad, in 1955. He writes in Arabic and French, and has published one collection in French and two in Arabic. He left Iraq for Beirut in 1979, later moving to Libya, then to Algeria. Since 1981 he has lived in Paris. He has translated works of two Iraqi poets, Mohammed Said Saggar and Abdelrahman Tuhmazi into French.

More rare

more rare
than a bird stumbling
on its shadow
than an ant lying in wait for
its prey,

more rare
than a raven
with white wings,

more rare
than a tornado
enveloped in my arms,
than a mutinous stick,
than a docile flame,

more rare
than all that

is to find myself
at peace for a moment

Word

In the word
uttered out of fear
I ask only for my silence

I demand a language to my measure

an eye
as wide as the desert

to speak to you about
what the poem does not say

and to make you see
what God
has never seen

An offending look

Like a desire interred
on the face of a drowned child
the desire to entrust the bridges
with the tangled banner and the river
with the sturdy calvary

I do not want to speak
of this nightmare
with everything in its place
the river bank and the river
nor of that prisoner
whom I took
for one of my brothers

I say nothing of
the Tigris parched of water
or the Euphrates

without residence permit

I say nothing
of the North abandoned
to its fate
nor of the South delivered
to its destiny

I say nothing of all that
but I speak of Sumer
which had on its conscience
remains of speech
of Babel
that guards in its memory
of the Gods
a devil's remorse

I also speak to you
of me
who casts on this view
of the past
an offending look

My city

on tiptoe
I would roam the world
and keep time
from its lugubrious air
and age
from these licentious years

I want to dig a trench
and hide the earth
from its mutilated heights
and the tree
from its scanty branches

I want to strip the desert
of its obscene skin
and the mirage of its chimera

I want to upset
rocambolesque nations
where amnesiac ardour flourished
and that squander
the plagues
of war

I want the clapped-out nights
of canicular blasts
and days maculated
with valetudinarian moments

I want to go
to the ends of the earth
to find the trace
of its footsteps
riddled by my shadow

I want to go
to the depths of the deep
and collect water in a colander
on the summit of the sun
and protect myself with a sieve

I want to become extravagant
so as to be able to tell you

I love you

Translated from the French by James Kirkup

Amel Moussa

Amel Moussa was born in Tunis. She has published two collections of poems, some of which have been translated into Spanish and Italian. She works as a journalist on *al-Sabah*, a Tunisian daily newspaper.

A formal poem

In the old house
where my grandfather composed his formal poems
I live as a concubine in my kingdom,
my dress is wet,
and on my head I place a crown.

In the old house
where the jug is tilted
water seeps out
mixed with prayers.

In the old house
where my first cry echoed,
I spread the soil of lineage
for us to sleep on,
one soul stacked next to another.

In the old house
where my grandmother was throned a bride
I search for her shawl
and place it for my shoulders to kiss.

In the old house
I cross ancient nights
and carry food to dervishes.

In the old house
I hand away my embers as a dowry
to lovers bathing in rain.

In the old house
Love wears us like a cape
and the courtyard becomes
twice its size.

Female of water

Water did not rush our way
burning with the ferocity of thirst.

Why does water follow in my tracks
and forget its channels
and flood plains?

Why do I not rest my face
at the edge of the water
to know
how it hid its colour from us,
how we made it lose its scent?

Why do I not become the secret of water?
Why do I not become female to its male,
and wait for him in the jug
until summer arrives.

My mother

I wrap her in cotton.
I plant her in my bosom,
my suckling first born,
my mother.
She wraps me in a foliage
of nakedness.

She pats away my shivers.
In her hands yesterday's scars
are healed.

Love me

I carry me on my fingertips.
I carry me on the galloping of my vision.
I wrap myself with a swaddling of my skin.
I embrace me, longing for myself.
I bless my flowing, my gushing.
I cradle me in my chest.
I glove these budding hands with poetry.

I claim revelation,
my engravings are on stone.
My image carries water to thirst,
and bait to fishermen's nets.
I spend the tolling of evening bells
sculpting.
I sleep in my own shade.
I wear my Bedouin nature
to spite cities.

I stroll within me
when I weary myself.
I enter a garden
that does not entice myself against me.
I love my impossible self,
the one whose feet
the earth does not know.

Desires of a mad mind

Whenever these feet dance
my memory besieges me

and pants ahead of me
demanding my dowry.
But my dowry
        is a poem:
        the impossible head of death.

On every journey
I lose my ring;
the sapphire stone
        falls.

In every migration
solitude bites my nails,
and I return
crawling.
My knees carry me
toward my island.
I ask the sailor for my ring.
I search in houses for a pillow
that holds my mind's desires.

Translated by Khaled Mattawa

Saadia Mufarreh

Saadia Mufarreh graduated from Kuwait University in Arabic language and education in 1987, and now works as arts editor of *al-Qabas* daily newspaper in Kuwait, as well as writing for other Arab newspapers and magazines. Since 1990 she has published four collections of poetry, the latest in 1999.

Electra

This ambiguous being
where the humming of truth blends
with the sweetness of myth,
and the expected poem
with memories whose heroic images are overblown
and where there is . . .
a lonely photograph that
I stand in front of as if it's a mirror
whenever the hidden questions multiply
and sneak towards me
from the holes in the family tales
amputated by necessity.

Refrigerator

I opened it,
its contents were tidy.
Bottles of preserved milk
cartons of yogurt
bags of frozen meat
yellow apples
medicine and bread
and . . . and . . . etc.
In the refrigerator of my soul

the contents scatter
and expire
and no one opens them.

The mirror lying down

The gardens he has been persistently painting
have no trees, or rivers of milk and honey running through.
The spaces in the gardens he paints
can only be pale blue
as if they are mirrors lying on their backs
looking at a sky clouded with trees that are stingy
with their early ripened fruit.

A broken glass

He mixes his colours
whenever he notices two eyes worth painting,
or the hem of a coloured dress
or the beak of a dove
or even a broken glass.

He makes hasty brush strokes on the white haze
in front of him, challenging
whenever the skies look wider
and the distinguishing features
are further apart from each other.

He paints
whenever his chest beats with bottled-up sorrow.

To Fadwa Tuqan

Right in her
something lives.
It takes a carnival of wisdom as a ritual,
it sits on a throne of femininity and questions
called amazement.
Its features sketch a full moon
behind ashes of clouds
and in the presence of trees.

To Mahmoud Darwish

Where incidents walk the same road
and the words ride together along the banks of first
    questions,
where there are many declared attempts
at suicide by linguists and grammarians,
and the children on the boring school chairs
learn how to draw poetry
and pride themselves in words and sounds
and sometimes succeed.
Where "The Lonely Horse . . . " stands
lonely . . . to a certain extent,
enemies of poetry bad-mouth it behind its back
and the last poet becomes
as if he has never been!

Oh . . . God!

Translated by Nay Hannawi

Khaled Najar

Khaled Najar was born in Tunis in 1949. He has travelled widely in Europe and the Arab world, and is a travel writer for Arab newspapers. He is one of the most lyrical of Tunisian poets; however, he resists publication and only one volume of his work has been published in Arabic, from which these translations have been made.

Stone castle

In the windows of sand
in death
in a chalk-drawn circle
in castle walls

your liquid name, beloved,
was an old journey,

      a song
that comes with the wind to my house in winter.

It was the lantern of the orchards
long dimmed by the tide.
It returned
as a moon above the banks of death
and in its waning reflected
lights from the islands.
They remain at the bottom of the river
to celebrate a feast for my sorrow by the walls
of Mary Magdalene's home.

It was my face
and my stone castle.

Boxes

They stole my childhood from me
and my madness.
They stole my winds
from the wooden crates
where I kept my clothes.
And from the gates of the South
they stole the croaking of my frogs
and my mother's mirrors.

Poem 1

And I return to the old house from travel.
Things regain their old taste
and their sad silence.
At night I will walk by my loved one's windows
the way autumn passes by
because the wind still brings back the bitterness
of old days
and takes from the sand
all that we said
the day you first saw me.

Poem 2

Like the sun under water
your face,
like time
a crucifix in my night.
In the memory of days,
lakes from a star
bring the wind back to my house
and give me
our childhood that died

the way butterflies die
in a summer without shores.

Poem 3

When I was young
I walked to the gates of the South
listening to the gushing of springs at night.
When I was young and innocent
like the shells of dreams,
the butterflies on the roof were my stars
and the shadows of horse carts
were my angels.

Poem 4

Across the bridge
an angel passes sobbing.

Poem 5

I hold a candle and flowers
in the silence of my hand.
I hold a mirror, a sock, a cloud
in the silence of my hand,
and your singing is lost
in a distant summer
among parafin lamps.

I hold a notebook and doors
and the sea,

and butterflies
and the sadness of eternity.

Snowflakes

Like the flint glass of old lanterns
without colour or glow,
like the sorrows of autumn,
I become when you arrive
shaking the gates of my heart,
placing snowflakes on my eyelids.
In the silence of the dark
I hear the wind howling
at the porthole
and my pulse, trembling
with sorrow, weeps.

And I am made naked by your eyes.

Mail 1

In the city there is
an empty street
and a lit window.
You are there
every evening waiting
for mail that will not arrive.

And you weep.

In the city there is . . .

Mail 2

In the city there is
an empty street
and a window where you can be seen
sewing

the cold fringes of sadness and death.
Every evening you are framed in it
waiting
for mail that will not arrive.

In the city there is . . .

Translated by Khaled Mattawa

Hassan Najmi

Hassan Najmi was born in 1959 in Ibn Ahmed, Morocco. He has a diploma in Arabic literature from Rabat College of Literature and Humanities. In 1977, his work began to be published in various newspapers. He has published four collections of poetry, one novel and two books of essays, one with Moroccan artist Mohamed Kacimi. He is an editor of *al-Ittihad al-Ishtiraki* daily newspaper and president of the Moroccan Union of Writers.

The four seasons

Roses side by side.
They don't speak to each other.

And these seasons alternate over my body,
they don't speak to each other
and they don't speak to me.

And I am here without a voice
speaking to all things
and not speaking to myself.

The window

Nothing remains:
only the wound of memory.
And the meeting place.
The smell of the paper of used books.

From the window:
a song about an ancient love.

As if to write the book of the dead,
night becomes his habit.

As if to entertain
a sadness that accompanies him
he dances alone at night.

The exiled

To Abbas

Their palms are coffins
and their heads are hats for distant clouds.
And behind them there is time
without flowerpots
        or arms

They had left.
And leaving itself returned.
And still they did not come back.

A small woman

On a rainy night she stood crying.
Like defenceless rain she wept.
I did not lift my eyes from the book.
And I did not wipe her tears.

Before I lay to sleep
she appeared in the last chapter of the novel.

So as not to cry
I closed the book, my head on the pillow.

The bar

In the neighbourhood bar
I saw my shadow drinking
a glass of wine.

And I am here
overtaken by drunkenness
as my words stumble.

The blueness of evening

I desire other places to see you in
grass to rest on
and a thirsty tongue
to drink with and to name you.
I desire night.
I desire another settlement to my days.
And I desire you.

In the blueness of evening, oh how much I desire
and how much do I not desire . . .

Ah, and this shiver coming
with the night clouds!

The train yard

A woman tourist in the station. A kiosk for newspapers, and
tobacco. A depressing newspaper. A small corner in the bottom
of the page for forgetting. Two hands with an extinguished
cigarette. Blown nerves. Clouds in the faces. A closed shop.
Police news bubbling in newspapers. Police that corrupt cities.
A crime in the garden. Half-naked bodies for the camera of the
superintendent. Two lovers on the right sidewalk. Bare legs. A
maid pours a bucket of water by the entrance. A guard dozes

off at the entrance of a building. An advertising poster on the
school gate. The remains of leaflets in the dirt beneath. A
window without a curtain. An evening of nervousness. A
nervousness hidden in the screens inside people's homes.
Programmes for health awareness. A religious sermon. Chatter
at the post office. A woman complains about her neighbour. A
girl on the balcony in her nightgown. A silhouette walks to his
bed. A dirty newspaper cut-out. An admirable rising. A
striking-up of friendship. Entwining grass. Emotions filling.
Speeches by sycophants. Compensations for bribery.
Immunities without immunity. The deviations of an era.
Distortions without end. Silence seeping from human pores.
Dead cities. Cities-Cemeteries. . .

> My cup and I
> I hoodwink my shadow
> In Ibn Batuta's café.
> Where are you?
> You didn't come?
> . . . .
> O how heavily night settles
> in my body

Couplets

In the light of your eyes
no light can save me but the lamp of my body.

With what legs can I join your dance
while all my body's flutes are dumb?

Why did words pour?
And the pouring of silence . . .
how can I erase it from my body?

Everything in me is erased if I am erased.
Nothing remains after the body's erasure.
Except this: My body.

N. A.

An evening passes toward your night
the way noon crosses though a song.
You do not tire.
as if you did not have a body.
And time shivers by your soul
as if you awaken light from its sleep

At night
here you are again stripping a sky of its stars.

The war

I send for a safe place
for my mother's scent
and hide the rose in my blood.

Silently
my mother came to me in sleep.
She kissed my forehead
and sprinkled salt under the pillow.

Electrocuted sky.
And the ground is sprouting
with the martyr's blood.
I see my mother's face.
I saw it on the train that passed today
loaded with the dead.

Translated by Khaled Mattawa

Amjad Nasser

Amjad Nasser was born in 1955 in al-Turra, Jordan. From 1976 he worked as a television and newspaper journalist, and for the arts section of *al-Hadaf* journal in Beirut. Later, in Cyprus, he was arts editor of *al-Ufq* magazine. Since 1987 he has been arts editor of *al-Quds al-Arabi* daily newspaper in London. He has published seven collections of poetry and one travel book. Three volumes of selected poetry have also been brought out; one in Cairo in 1995, a second by the House of Poetry in Palestine, and in 1998 a selection in French, introduced by Adonis and translated by Adnan Mohsen.

Hope's front

Hope is yet another night from whose front
dawn's scouts have not yet returned.
I've waited.
But the sign,
the first glimmer of light,
the waving of the hand –
has lost the way.

Watchtower

Under your watchtower I stand
between the commanding eye and the arrow.
A sign could bring my end,
another could bring me to life.
Confusion alone could help me out.
Shorter than the sister's joy, a hand stretches out to me,
and I raise my hand, just like that, toward an unmarked day.

Three signs on the blind's way

I
How could a light person like me carry
the two loads: Sign and Secret?
That's why I sway.

II
My wandering sight has seen far and near
but not the white on my temples.
Is that what makes me blind?

III
The first told me about spring;
the second about summer;
but the third parted
with her two little feet a path
in the middle of September's harvest.
All three
told all that's motionless on earth:
Walk gently!

IV
Three larks were startled
by the stride of the blind.
The pit listened on the sly.

V
The three signs which crossed
my way pointed toward the mountain.
But I headed toward the valley.
Shortsightedness?

VI
From the diwan of al-Suhrawardi
fell three drops of blood.
The noon's horizon
a red-skinned rose.

VII
The three Magi,
who ride the wind through the nights,
saw a lone star on the west horizon.
The wooden cross is budding.

Translated by Anton Shammas

Once upon an evening, in a café

When your thoughts
don't take you too far
and you are silent
as you tremble
and gaze
at the trellis of your hands.

When the chariot of your imagination
does not lead you into tunnels
lit up with apprehensions
and lightnings
as you remain silent
and tremble
gazing at the smoke twirling
around your wrist.

When the woman who lets
her scarf fall
through the evening's emptiness
greets you, and you don't
    acknowledge
her greeting, but rather
remain silent, and tremble
as you gaze
at the destinies that unfold, lurching
in your coffee cup.

When the new immigrants pass by
arm in arm with their local women
blabbering about time that flees
so soon, and you keep silent
as you tremble and gaze
at the table's
ambiguous wood.

When you don't sit with anyone
and remember war only
as a horseshoe, or a coat
riddled with bullets.

When, upon an evening, in a café
the faces pass by you
like copper clouds
as you listen
to cymbals that chime
in a far-away desert
or masts that break
in imaginary gulfs.

When the blind singer's
record spins, once upon an evening,
in a café, the customers sigh
and you walk toward the axe
where it leans against the tree.

Bakunin's fish

The anarchist woman
who makes the air quake
when she speaks;
who lets her hair down
like a field of bell peppers;
who stares a man down
in anger, and leads a horde
of extremist views;

who rises amid coffee cups
and low tobacco clouds
to terminate a discussion with a violent gesture;
who tries to string together
Bakunin's wild fish with one thread
of high-wired sarcasm;
who comes from the bastions of ideology
to furnish the middle of the 19th century
with a window of wasps;
the anarchist woman
who came from Gütenburg
to the capital of Tunisia,
met a date-palm from the East
and was turned into a date.

Offering

I remember no scent of yours
that lingered on my neck,
or lurked in my shirt wrought of kisses,
nor a voice that would remain
after your halo had raced you to the door.

With tears you never shed before
you thoroughly washed the glass;
the paper towels that wiped the life-water
off our legs, ended up
with cigarette butts and apple peels
in the waste basket.

And that red spot you discovered on the bedsheets
in the morning, was only a sign
that the offering had been accepted.

Wildernesses

How will I write my poem
when I have nothing
but the wreckage of description?
How will I prepare
my florid blurry praise
for the princess's face
in its white quietude?
How will I pursue
the gazelle's trail
shot through with golden shards?

I went down to the river
and found nothing but pebbles
and the commandments of drought.
I went to the lovers;
and found only the ink of letters
the autumn of cloves.
I went to the wilderness
and found only the wolf's solitude,
loneliness of the serpent.
I went to wisdom
and found nothing but
the leftovers of a sermon.

I went
to poetry
and found nothing
but the wreckage
of description.

Translated by Sargon Boulus

Salwa al-Neimi

Salwa al-Neimi was born in Damascus, Syria. She has lived in Paris since the mid-1970s, where she studied Islamic philosophy and theatre at the Sorbonne. In 1980 she published her first collection of poetry. Then in 1981 she started working as a journalist for Arab magazines and newspapers, and stopped writing poetry. But in 1994 she published a collection of short stories, followed, in 1996 and 1999, by two further collections of poetry.

Old follies

I used to sleep like the murdered.
Now I sleep like a murderer.

Between subject and object
my body swings.

My mother taught me a great deal.
I discovered my solitude on my own.
Between a man I strap to my bed
and a man I leave standing at my doorstep
my laughter shifts.

My father flirted with my mother.
My sister with the neighbours' boy.
My brother with his girlfriend in college.
I flirted with them all
(but no one noticed me).

I didn't think my sister was telling the truth
(she lied ravenously)
when she told me about her lover
until I smelled his body with my own nose.

His golden crotch shone in the sun.
Is it enough that his crotch shine

for my lust to overflow?

To you, whom I loved, goodbye.
Through you I reached my great love (of myself).
To you I loved: I still love you.

I do not need a broom.
I wait quietly
for my wings to grow.
But I need the scent to start wafting
and for the words to finish me.

The scent of desire and words of pleasure.
Does this mean I'm a speaking animal?

Final scene

The serious man analyses
the election results
and ponders the prices
of women's underwear.
The other one places his watch
in front of him
and desires me
with all the lust of all the men he imagines
in my bed
And the one who stood at the edge of the torrent
was asleep and is now back.

And I?
I spin around myself
alone in the huge bowl.
I mature quietly
and shout victory chants
and cries of conquest.

Translated by Khaled Mattawa

Salah Niazi

Salah Niazi was born in 1935 in Nasiriyah, Iraq, and has lived in Britain since 1963. He was educated at the Baghdad Teachers' Training College and at the School of Oriental and African Studies, London. From 1965 to 1984 he worked for the BBC Arabic Service. He is a poet and critic, and founder editor of the quarterly Arabic literary journal *al-Ightirab al-Adabi*. He has published six volumes of his poetry. Recently he translated Shakespeare's *Hamlet* and *Macbeth*, and is currently working on James Joyce's *Ulysses*. The work below is the sixth and final part of *Facades of Spain*, an epic poem on the rise and fall of civilisations in three phases. In the first phase the rivers are a cradle for civilisation. In the second, (the Middle Ages), the sea is the means to conquer the world, and the present phase is that of the wind (or sky) which carries pollution and recognises no man-made borders.

The wind

I am your lord,
And I am on the throne alone,
There is no god but me.
I am the shooting stars,
The clouds are my men,
And my ready troop of horse.
I am the end,
The decisive hour.
I roam the ends of the earth
I steal into every cradle.

I am the wind,
Ice shivers at my approach
I make mothworms eat into steel.
I am like a mummy, which woke up without a head,
And staggered unconscious,
Trying to look around,
I bring pollution, acid rain, radiation and ashes.

The Sufi* cries: "God is within my jubbah"
But I slip into underwear,
Get into the bottles of medicine.
I get into the darkest corners,
The insides of dummies and dolls.
I pass contagion from one lung to the other,
From one border guard to the other.
I carry the scent of every crime,
While Eliot cries: "Clear the air!
Clear the sky! Wash the wind!"

The sea woke up and smote the land,
New worlds came into being,
And others came to an end,
New forms of taking life came about.
Whoever creates a new tool of destruction rules supreme
This is the way of the world.

Well done, kingdoms of the earth!
Well done, kingdoms of the sea!
I am the wind, there is no god but me,
I am the shooting stars,
The clouds are my men and troop of horse.

I am a god without a creed,
I am the malady, and the microbes of infection
And death is my merciful treatment
Above my spheres hover dark satellites,
Electronic antennae and atomic feelers,
Ingenious ways of killing have been devised
And whoever discovers a new tool of destruction rules
    supreme
This is the way of the world.

My rain is acid rain,
Which carries decay to the roots,
To the potato tubers,
And leaves fish floating like miniature coffins.

---

* The name given to adherents of pantheistic mysticism in Islam.

From country to country I drive the poisonous clouds
As from this day boundaries have disappeared
And secure boundaries are a striving after wind
All maps are the scrawls of wearied children,
I am the boundaries
I drive poisonous clouds from land to land
And smite all beings with numbness and delirium,
So that a lover has no interest in his beloved,
And even bulls are incapable of butting.

In my name battles are fought
And in the name of pollution wars are declared.

I can see the populations of whole countries emigrating
Seeking a breathing space,
In a remote corner.

Today the sea is out of bounds,
Although the search for undiscovered islands continues
Tomorrow all homelands will be out of bounds
Gas masks will be let on a daily basis like videos.
And oxygen jars paid for by instalments.
Package holidays will be arranged to other air pockets,
In a forgotten desert land
Or some cave high up in the mountains,
Airlines are discovering new resorts where breathing is
   possible.
I can see the populations of whole countries emigrating
To remote deserts, and high inacessible caves
Package tours to start with,
At reduced rates to start with,
Crowds will then gather as in ant-hills in the high caves
And I the mighty polluted god
Impatient of waiting
Stand at the door.

Translated by Jareer Abu Haidar

Mostafa Nissabouri

Mostafa Nissabouri was born in 1943 in Casablanca. He gave up his
university studies in order to find work and, as one of the poets in
Morocco to question established poetics, co-authored the 1964
manifesto "Poésie toute". In 1966 he co-founded the revue *Souffles*
and, in 1971, *Intégral*, which was run by the painter Mohamed Melehi.
In 1968 Nissabouri published a volume of poetry entitled *Plus haute
mémoire*, and in 1975 his collection *La mille et deuxième nuit* was a
sellout. In 1997 he published *Casablanca, fragments d'imaginaire*, and
in 1999 the joint collection *Aube* and *Approche du désertique*. He writes
in French, and lives and works in Casablanca.

from Approche du désertique

1
Your land when it surfaces
in orphaned syllables
that land is granted rights to a patrimony of absence
so untenable is it between two reveries
it wraps itself in reverberations from the plain
and there is a cypress on the slope of a hill
to measure itself against the equilibrium of the horizon
so that time may far and wide
remain forever immobile

But you in the middle
standing in the affinity of tombs
it is as if you were still
the same anonymous traveller
the traveller you say has long been prepared
for the gravity of observation of dunes
he who has something like a revisited shadow
within his profoundest weft and warp
his essential prolongations
and who has seen that ambivalent structure's

perspective in fragmentation
its field of unknowing
engaged in a vagabond latitude
the desertified pleadings when the body
can no longer lay claim to belonging

Others have shadows on the earth
analagous with matter light and space
without pursuing to the frontiers
of all dissemblances

Then there comes to you desire to circumscribe here and
   now
the ultimate metaphor in words that amalgamate
confusedly the positions of the stars
with stumbling blocks of denegations
that situate approximately the axis
reserved for the occultation of its own matter
under a sky remaining linked to a telluric disorder
wherein each place has preserved
an immutable moon incorporated
as a sovereign incrustation
from an ineffable metric of the desert

Metaphor deriving from conifer and oleander
that they may stand together forming
a portico for examinations of the stars
starting with trees producing from among their branches
an eruption of remembering
endowing memory at each step
in conformity with the exuberance of dunes
with bygone vows the oaths of expiation
mingling with attacks on the prodigious
incessant communion between notebooks of wanderings
and incidentally a surrection of incorruptible calligraphies
perpetuating in their romance
some rhetoric of desire
hidden away behind the tufts of marrubium

metaphor that equals forgetting
all at once the palms
with their almost desperate majesty
of silhouettes inclined over imaginary maps
even as the town at the centre that assigns to the clouds
the light incarnation of its sepulchres
displayed above the red and mauve minarets
a perfect itinerary of storks
a town where so many times one wished
to sleep to die then resuscitate before departing thence
for while there remained between the lips
no more than an itinerant interrogation of stone
a woman at dawn would come to withdraw the shroud
prepare with residual inks
the electuary that delivers
from introversion of clepsydras

and the sea entire losing its way within without
in the immensity of the body and the canyons of its cry
with those alphabet cargoes of neutralised consonants
that acclimatise childhood by invading it
from already premeditated origins

a sea where the ships with their cut-out hulls
all gleaming with the blood from slashed veins of sirens
make a link between sleep and wake
without one's even knowing if they drift towards the shore
or if it is the shore trying to reach them
like a coincidence of foams within a country
that never stops encountering itself again
losing itself retrieving itself and again losing itself
each time inscribed in a decisive finality before
being vested in words that have not been spoken
fragments of words still imbued with their silences
the gloss of the very sediments in books
bound by parchment and azure dreams
to the extinct constellations

2
Voyage in which are re-invented
topographies deserted by their south

first of all
an unfinished expanse
presence bordering on
hypothetical regions
of an unrecalled identity
and about to overflow
at this moment
in the new amended interrogation's
thorough-going exegesis

all incumbent upon me the ash
from a sky glimpsed withdrawing
into the densities of pseudonym
the riverside established
from here to the mnemonic
when the moon
has a tarnished gloss
of oracular bones
that under the moonlight
of statues are up to the knees in water
parodying these times' penury of angels

and under the precariousness of clouds
all the constraint of landscape
just as it fell to the lot
of the suspended morning's
first taking flight

3
Here is another sky
preeminence of elsewhere
on the thoroughfares of the vocable
like resorption of azure
serving as anchorage
for the anterior body

like an instant of high rapture
that re-invents a language and sets it out of reach
confronting a point of simulation in the plain
of obscure funeral processions
confronting a network of lanes
tented in an indentation of the real
confronting the primacy of the possible and the probable
on imaginary confines
it one day was reflected in my soul
absorbing its texture
before its ultimate dissociation in cloud

another sky
with all these hours
cystallising in the abdomen
and charged with the final flux
of a potential hieroglyph
to be communicated later
with its nuances of gemlike salt

with what remains
constantly traversed
from the recesses of this somnambular matter
because it situated the lost land
at the estuary of dreams
its euptions of jujube trees
its bronze persistence
of eternity
in fragmentary illumination

with this absence
arrived on the threshold of hyperbole
engaging the shadow on an earth
that unawares becomes delimited
with limewashed stones and spergulas
where there is barely enclaved
a supposed clearing
almost the place to conceive oneself
without dwelling without memory
without evocation even of a possible return

into another time
its night a catafalque hoisted
on denuded shoulders
finally to accede
to the recitation that alternates
stars and suns seized in the ice
of this very inscription
where this cosmicity falls silent
simply intermediary reality
for a joint ownership of landscape
with its already defunct genealogies
and to hold itself at a distance
reliquary of scattered night
in places of self-denying errancy.

4

The sky's peculiarity
is to recover
the ample field of wakening
somewhere
magic of blue surfacing
in dense theorems
what is needed is an environment
like the Sea of Crises
to detect in the roses of sand
so many concretionary otherwheres
in the neurons of air

each place is rendered
more essential
with its play of shadow
on the surface
with words that are no more than
gleanings of dreams
dramatised reflections where the sun is incarnated
invariably dreamed-of death
finally re-editing its description of the day-star
of words with whatever remains
of language
on arbitrary peninsulas

of fables begun once again
with emergence
cumulus cut-outs
with inseparable profiles
of a vain anteriority

it is the same voyage
that does not want to end
founded in a mechanism
of episodic territories
in which proportionately withdraws
the forgetting of roots
and that engages during brief mornings
the excesses of geography
to remain in the middle immobile
producing a parcellisation of dead steppes
in which the sky is agglutinated
without being the centre of all circumnavigations

wherein the equivocality of day is tremblingly seized
in a marine recession
where to associate its quest
and the sense of repetitive debris
there are marginal grounds with
continuous revelation
of the same refractory land
that would like a neighbouring of eternity
disengaged from distant extramdauras
captured in the void of the retina

heights remaining dominated
by the inks of remembrancings
and which I must endow with
space gravity phenomenal matter
ordering of the horizon and the course
outdated of the idioms I bear

Translated by James Kirkup

Saif al-Rahbi

Saif al-Rahbi was born in 1956 in Suroor, Oman. He left Oman as a teenager to study in Cairo. After working there for a few years, he travelled to Damascus, Algiers, Beirut, Sofia, London, Paris and The Hague. In London he was a journalist on the literary magazine *Awraq*. When he returned to Oman in 1994, he established *Nizwa*, now Oman's major quarterly arts magazine. Ten volumes of his poetry, prose and essays have been published.

Nothing started

Everything has started!
Nothing has started!
Thus I start!
Thus, forever,
the ibexes of the self
die in the meadows of yelling.
Thus wars break out in which
the ships of thought sink.
The ships of thought sink,
and thus I dream of being
an orchestra conductor
on islands
blazing with fires.

Those who were

You used to pass by our days
and touch the blossoms
that dew of words
and those songs.
You were an anniversary of joy's resurrection
and horizons that call for their murdered ones

whenever night descends.
You were courage's right hand
and birds of desire swooping
down a mountain slope of a morning
and you were, just now,
"builders of solitude"

From the room to the café

In the morning when I wake up,
the world wakes in my head
with creatures and screams that smash my bones.

I leave my room
that's like a cave filled with the slain,
and shuffle off to the café.
I look sharply at my cup that's like a snake
relaxing on a summer afternoon,
and think: "This is my last cup in this city!"

But morning is still at its outset,
and I'll go through wars and kisses
and only discover their flavour
after centuries.

Bells will not toll tonight

The storm in front of my door
will not subside tonight.
Its Herculean armies have slammed the door of sides.

In the churches' fading light
I glance at monks pulling handcarts,
fleeing to the mountains
on horses that stretch and strain in the wind
as if from the Byzantine age.

On this memorial night,
bells will not toll,
the storm will never subside.

A prayer

This night is unbearable,
With its heavy axes and blades that sink into my heart.
This country is unbearable,
O Allah, take it a while from my shoulder,
from the horn of the bull you left carrying the rock,
wandering in the wilderness,
neither dead nor alive,
the lightning of agony oozing from its stony eyes.

Take this rock a while,
this earth,
this egg that floats in orbit,
this glass, empty of its liquor.

O Allah,
Take it a while from me,
we are not its worthy inheritors.

Our old house

It's as if I'm walking
through valleys, filled with fear,
valleys I can neither touch
nor easily recall.
As if I'm taking that first step there,
I walk into our old house, and find emaciated horses,
with the ghosts of our ancestors
wandering amongst their neighings.

The door opens onto this desert of absence

a smell of grilled fish,
a smell of gas, wafting
from the disused stove.

The jars as they were, speaking to the corners,
and water still boiling in the pots.
The sheep are back from the fields
except for the one a wolf ate.
Saddles and guns hang on the walls
as if at a funeral gathering.
Tomorrow is Eid al-Adha*,
but the children have forgotten to buy new shoes,
or wash their feet before they slept.

White clouds wrap the neighbouring sky,
and accompany travellers to their distant villages.
And we are swimming in the festival rain,
where birds gently peck the air,
to wake it, with us, on the roofs,
where we dried our dates and dreams
on the clayey balconies
and fell between the feet of an agitated bull,
where the stains of an enervated sun
seize the house, with its birds and women
and ancient trees stumbling like
shepherds among ruins.

Beyond the fence
you can still see the palm trees,
like bewildered spirits colliding with minarets,
like ships lowering their sails
in misty seas,
and amid their somnolence and green dreams
lurks the evening's next soirée.

---

* the Sacrifice Festival.

Dostoyevsky's garden

With a pale cloud, Raskolnikov enters
his cave, armed with stones,
a garden in which darkness festers,
where the knife takes its course,
softly, into the entrails.

A letter whose owner might have died
the day before
and a carpet where insects play.

He explores the star of lineages
on the hand of a whore
and listens to the soul weeping beneath the shoes.
Thus, always, a childhood strangles its birth
with a stroke of an axe,
and the room is the desert of the worshipper.

Steps

I walk, I feel under my feet
a sky, trembling with all its victims,
and on my head, an earth
that has stopped rotating.

I hear a thunder of steps behind me,
steps of people coming
from the past,
silent as if they are dead.
Past, retreat a while,
let me finish today's walk.

Arrival

When I travel to a country,
rumours precede me there,
and I am aroused
like a wolf whose fantasies anticipate
its prey,
and I never arrive.

Music

When I go out,
I leave the music on
to guard the souls of the dead,
music of the ancients that carries
the smell of grass,
and guards the gardens of Babylon
hanging in the depths.
When I go out,
I leave everything closed in on itself
except for the music throbbing in the empty lounges
and some oysters,
which I picked from the shore
on the night of the storm.

Translated by Abdulla al-Harrasi

Fuad Rifqa

Fuad Rifqa was born in 1930 in Kafroun, Syria, and graduated from the American University of Beirut and Tübingen University, Germany, later spending some years in the USA. In the late 1950s he co-founded *Shi'r* poetry magazine with Youssef al-Khal and Adonis. He has lived in Lebanon for many years and is Distinguished Professor of Arabic philosophy at the American University of Beirut. He has published numerous collections of poetry, and is an important translator into Arabic of Rilke, Hölderlin and other German authors.

A spark

In his poem
a trembling spark
It brushes his eyelashes,
stretches them to a horizon that recedes
In a fog it disappears
behind the dots, the commas, and the letters

Sadness

In his right hand, the sun ferments
In his left, the moon turns green
In his heart
        the princess of love.
And oh, this sadness,
this dark-leafed sadness.
Why?
From where?

Yeast

At Earth's limit
his feet, always.
Towards the other side
he extends bridges he doesn't cross.
In the ferment of his limbs:
>   the waters of the fields
>   the fragrance of blossom's
>   and Sun's flower.

In the rising leaven of his being
the ringing call of life to life.

Siesta

Under an olive tree
at pasture's edge
a cow half asleep,
on her back a grey bird
pecking at his neck.
>   In his feathers
Red Indian braids.

A glance

Through the crack in the wound
he cleanses the sky.
From the sun's rays
he weaves his cloak.

A thought

Between his eyes and her tears
this suitcase, always packed
and the distances of so many journeys
    to see
    to feel the fire of poetry
               in a foreign land

A garden

Fence and walls,
under the vineyards
oblivious to harm,
the guard stays awake.
    And at night
without knocking at the door
without stumbling
Autumn sneaks into the trees
fills its sacks with fruits
and hides beneath the leaves.

(A voice from the clouds)

Pray and keep watch,
no one knows
when the thief may come.

Edge

At the edge of existence
    forever he stands
    a ticket in his pocket
He waits for the ship
and the signal flag

Night of the world

He casts his nets
into the caverns of whales
He raises the masts
lights the lanterns
and shatters apart
Into the night of the world.

Surprise

A spring night
A moon round with health
Beneath a gladsome rock,
a stream murmurs
And yet
they ask him:
"What's up with you?
Why don't you speak?"

A wish

For the hungry
        that his poem be
        bread and oil.
For the thirsty
        cool streams.
For the wandering
        home and lantern.

            For life
            that it be lilies and dew,
            that it be harvest.

Morning star

At night's end
Towards the morning star
he lifts his gaze
It spends the night alone
lighting windows.
He spends the night alone
opening windows.

Two friends
        the whole sky between them

Wedding

In the winter of his years
on a chair beside the window.
Through the cracks
the snow creeps over his feet,
buries them,
buries his waist and his neck,
and he doesn't move.

He knows
he is late for the wedding,
for all weddings.

Introduction

Endlessly you aim
towards a star
towards the pages of the poem
in your eyes, a cloud
from the pantings of the deep
from a new land.

But life tightens around you
and the poem
forever tempts you
and the lantern is broken
timeworn.

Oil lamp

Through the streambeds of darkness
through its cracks
A face always peers out,
approaches,
lights the oil lamp and whispers

His hand in mine
we head for mountain chains
and the flower of dusk.

At the edge of the tower

The childhood that loved him:
        in the riverbeds
The woman that loved him:
        in the darkness of roots
The friends that loved him:
        in the ships of ashes
The poems that loved him:
        in the tines of the pitchfork

        At the edge of the tower
        alone, he stands
        No hat, no coat

A prayer

A summer passes on
a bird flies away
wind blows
river rumbles
        night
embers stay awake
bread, wine
a hand offers thanks
a god watches over.

Oak tree

An oak tree over his head
wiping the sweat off his brow
stretching a mat for him
so he can sleep

In the morning it pulls off the blanket
He goes to his field,
he becomes the sickle and the plough.

And tomorrow
when he does not return
it dons its mourning clothes
drapes its hair with fog.

Wanderer

Wanderer,
all his travels
are in one direction

Arrow

Out from Earth's darkness
an arrow tears forth
In the air it quivers
catches fire
turns to ashes

Between him and that arrow
        an old friendship

Cloud

A white cloud
He's afraid
Will it fall?
Will the wind swish it away?
In the unknown corners of this Earth
It alone knows him
It alone closes his eyes
and shuts the door.

Dream gardens

He knows she is beyond distance
beyond the Dream Gardens
And yet
every morning he carries a bouquet
and at the gates of the city
he waits for the train

Translated by Paula and Adnan Haydar

Sharif al-Rubai (1943–1977)

Sharif al-Rubai was born in Baghdad, in 1943, and was one of Iraq's 1960s generation of poets. He left his country in the mid-sixties to work as a journalist in Jordan. He then lived in Syria, Lebanon and Cyprus, finally settling in London in 1990. His poetry has been published in many magazines and newspapers including *Mawaqif, al-Adab, al-Karmel, al-Safir, al-Quds al-Arabi* and *al-Hayat*. This excerpt from 'Ashes of Intimacy' was published in *Bareed al-Janoub* newspaper a few months before al-Rubai's sudden death in September 1997.

from The ashes of intimacy

You who lapse behind
    fingers of shyness
how can I reach you?
How can I make
    my fervent language
into a covetous field
    for our desired rose
when between us
        there is always a wall
a wall to perpetuate oblivion
    to interject the flow of yearning
    where we hang the wash
    of our allusive pleasures
a wall to shade us from the blaze
        of fear
a wall of silence we brandish
    in the face of certainty
looking forward, you and I,
    to the final opening
the moment of emergence
    like a double wakefulness
        of fire and remorse.

And yet
        on those same walls
dripping with doubt
we had carved a single heart
        for two lovers
claiming our way into surprise
or into a time we pondered
        with patience like
                a mirage
and time after time
        we fell to our knees
                before the past
asking forgiveness for sins
        we never committed –

How can I reach you?

        Such a question,
it keeps me sleepless
        it makes me always
steal a furtive glance through the dungeon
                of difficult loving
that is your presence in me,
lamenting like the poet
                of icy ages
the sun that had died

It wasn't love
        it wasn't a hut
    devoured by the fires
        of jealousy,
neither a treacherous certainty
that we had stood behind
        the wall
    of all circumstance
and wailed for our calamitous desire

You and I
        between us a wall always
a wall to perpetuate oblivion

a silence we can brandish in the face
                    of certainty
for we were never in love
the wall confronting us was nothing
         but white lies
suitable as excuses
         for our defeat
in the face of encroaching love.

London, February 1992

Translated by Sargon Boulus

Wadih Sa'adeh

Wadih Sa'adeh was born in Lebanon in 1948. Seven collections of his poems have been published. He was awarded a grant to translate one of them into English, under the title *A Secret Sky*. He lives in Sydney, Australia, where he works as a journalist.

Genesis

With what meagre space
remaining between his hands
he tried to reconstruct
a universe: with a tear,
he drew a star, a moon with a glance,
and with a single touch, a sun.

When he closed his eyes,
people commuted to their work
on the sidewalk of his eyelids.

A country

It took its name
from water
and started to flow
The foam we saw
riding the waves
was its people
The grass over the dunes
their ribs

A country
whose men all
had departed, and so

the women were wed
to trees

Life there

There she buried
her child, and waited
for years to lie beside him.
When finally
they lowered her down
into that soil,
She was only one day old
while he was already
an old man.

In the tunnel, in the bone

Soon time will end.
Winds are approaching the immense wall.
And there they will buckle under.
They pass quickly, and the race is over.
Finally the winds will rest.
Time cracked open. It hangs only from one stitch.
I await its decline, its resounding fall to earth.

Life begins on the last day.
Days are many, but life is meagre.

It is delayed from day to day. And when there's only one day
left, it rushes into it in its entirety hoping to live there ... in this
way life begins, just when it's ending. That's why life will never
be lived!

I've still one day left, what should I do?
Begin life? With what will I begin this life?
With whom? How? With what action or speech?

And if I happen to meet someone, what will I say to him?
With you, now, I will begin my life? And if I said this, and he
responded, how will I live a life I'm saying goodbye to? How
will I live the death of life?

I woke up very early. Those who will depart must wake up
very early to enhance their final days. They must witness the
dawn, at least, before they go.

In this room's space exist the splinters of humans who lived
thousands of years ago, whom I say goodbye to, and become
splinters like them.

I say goodbye to the pulse of planets that reaches me across
the vacuum of space from distant galaxies. The galactic
swishings, the dust of stars, the air born a million years ago
crossing silently an immense space in order to reach me.

I say farewell to gasping volcanoes, to the drizzle of far-away
swamps, to the picture, the chairs, the mirrors, the clocks, my
children's eyes, their shoes scattered carelessly on the floor. I
say goodbye to the waves that penetrate my body, to the
vibrations that come from the oldest place, the big bang!

Did I have to clash with myself all this time, and everything
else with me, in order to become a silent prey in the end? Wasn't
I able, a long time ago, to relieve this noisy world of one voice
at least?

The universe must rest. Voices must all become silent.
Oh, for some quiet!

I can't describe the day, I can't describe anything. Speaking is
nothing but betrayal. They don't speak on the last day. They
just shut up and leave.

Those hills were silent also. And we were, with the stirring of
sun and wind, the only sound.

But we, with that monotonous movement in the stillness of
death, had snared mysteries from the bones.

How were we, simple as we are, flung between the jaws of immensities, to invent places that would protect us? How were we able to continue until today! We were no mortals. But certain bones of cattle and dry sticks saved our lives. It wasn't life that protected us, but death.

We mixed our births with grass. And under those thin ears of wheat our land found a shade. We never wore clothes, or trinkets or bracelets. But our breath was our cloth and ornament. We were naked. We found warmth in the firewood born of our panting, which was dry, and so ignitable.

Under the reign of flame, we had many celebrations for which we selected many guest seats, within our pores.

Life was within our skin, not outside. Thus, we lived life in its secret hideout, in dimness, in the womb, before it was born.

Our celebrations were tended in our veins, not in public squares. Our habitation in the imagination of place. Our caravans in the head, not on the roads . . .

We lived the anti-birth: there was our childhood, our youth and old age. And we met life once, before the door of death.

During the war, my father looked for a bone in the wilderness to crush it with a stone and satisfy his hunger. From those crushed bones a number of children were born, among whom I was one. I was the son of a crushed bone.

Inside the bone a tunnel opens now, where there is a wilderness and animals, and where my father is walking again.

He walks, taking me with him, hand in hand, looking for a bone.

We walk in the heart of the bone, looking for it. When we saw it at last, we were already far away.

We had become two bones, in which there was a tunnel where people walked around looking for bones.

I walked in the bone tunnel. My father had put me at the invisible point in the folds, in the dusty emptiness, the primal mother of the life of bones.

I turn my head back now and look: to those lost in bone marrow, to the ones who stand on its pavements, to those who stretch out their hands seeking an exit, to the dead with the electricity of spirit, to those who look for a stone to crush their bone and eat it, to the ones who have just entered, and scarcely know what they are doing.

I turn my head back and look: when I cast the marrow out, I had opened my passage. Emptiness was the way. Emptiness was the stone.

My child sleeps close to me. I will not say goodbye to her. I shall go to death as if I were going out to bring her some candy. I shall go to death as if going to a shop.

I was a little boy when my father carried me in his arms to a shop. He entered and said: This is my son, give him some candy. All throughout that day, I played with a handful of sweets.

But why do I reminisce over my childhood like someone entering life when I'm actually leaving it? And what's the use of recalling it when there is no room even for a phantom? Whole populaces, even those that are extinct, still reside here. I stare out of the window hoping they will walk on my glance, and get out. This room's arteries must rest!

Those who got out, left their splintered eyes on the walls. Those who stayed, hung up the sheep of their breath and ate
. . . I'll be the one to walk on my glance through the window, and disappear.

Those days, which are gone now, were not more than practice for entering life. Life is mere practice for entering it. But it ends there, and we never enter.

What we live of life is that practice. We live only the pre-birth. In the arteries that are still unformed. In the featureless face. Inside the entrails' ethereal darkness. We live on the edge, between being and nothingness. At the door. And when we attempt to exit, we are shattered, like a heavenly body, in the abyss.

So I'm not speaking about a life. I'm not describing a birth, but its absence. I'm not writing about a light, but a darkness. Not remembering what was, but what was supposed to be . . . This supposition that may finally be what we call our life.

. . . And saying farewell to it, perhaps, the only certainty. A few more seconds and I shall have my first certainty!

I will celebrate my veins. I will welcome those who emerge suddenly from the void, and dance with them.

Then I'll go back to the bone. To my father's secret. To the tunnel. Cast aside the guts, smile and go on my way.

Translated by Sargon Boulus

Amina Saïd

Amina Saïd was born in Tunis in 1953 to a Tunisian father and a French mother, and has been living in Paris since 1978. She writes in French and has published eight volumes of poetry and two volumes of re-invented Tunisian folk-tales. In 1989 she was awarded the Jean Malrieu Prize, and in 1994 the Charles Vildrac Prize. She has translated, from English to French, a novel and short stories by the major Philippino writer Francisco Sionil Jose. She writes in French.

I was born on the shores

of the Sea of the setting sun
the deep green sea
the Sea of the Philistines
that washed on Carthage
the white interior Sea of the Arabs
whose horses swept along its banks

I grew up   algae   wave   fish
star with multiple branches
the first letter of the alphabet
etched on my brow

at seven I swam in black waters
along moon-traced pathlight
up to the country of limits
I took lessons on mirages
intemporal scribe
dedicated to handwriting the centuries
with ink from the indigo Sea

at nine in wonder I discovered a sunken city
surfacing I laid out my wings to dry on the dunes
I counted the stones before gathering them
I had two faces I lived in two worlds

At eleven I no longer spoke to anyone
yet a language was taking shape in my mouth
I was looking in silence for the secret of poetry
trying to define myself within the orders of clarity
under its white veil behind made-up eyelids
my city kept its mysteries
did not console itself for its lost beauty
the Sea Gate no longer opened on the wide
neglecting our most beautiful legends
we lived our days and our nights seated
around a marble fountain gone dry

at sixteen I had a solemn smile
of one who dreams of breaking away
I had two faces I lived in two worlds
marvellously immobile
blind sphinxes peopled my sand gardens
firebirds flew across the sky
fissures of silence in the slow day's working
with death as a horizon the Sea held us back
its Medusa thighs undulating under our fingers

we lived our days and our nights seated
around a marble fountain gone dry
the Sea Gate no longer opened on the wide
blind sphinxes peopled my sand gardens
when a palm tree was planted which soon caressed the
    clouds
I remained at its foot my eyes towards the sky
my grandmother appeared
it is a sign she said you will leave us
she gave the usual commendations
poured on green water after my footsteps
to have you come back she said
already I was at the other shore

at forty always inhabited by shadows
between past and future
I issue from my childhood and thus from nowhere else
I remember a night which was young

lived to the rhythm of the Sea
there was between the world and myself
so much space and yet so little
enchantment complicity
this was before the protracted agony of the planet
before the rent in the mask
I had two faces I lived in two worlds
facing the embrace of the blue horizon
I dreamt of undulations in the desert

I issue from my childhood and thus from nowhere else
which truth therefore remains to be discovered
other than each day's sun
other than the ebb of sand from my winged hand
the immense voice of the world
in the single weft
of an indulgent language which was given to me

I who keep coming back who keep leaving
each threshold crossed
I advance toward my demise toward the first day
solitude thus scoops itself out
as one explores the bottom of an empty well
– for darkness only for darkness
faced with oneself –
seeking the place where the reflection of light is found

praise for the one syllable sun
the archipelago of silence where I find my words
the voyage from threshold to threshold which is the real trip
praise to him who goes astray
he whose words are singular
praise for the world because everything exists
elsewhere than in the poem and in it too

still between past and future
I wanted to discover she who had to be
now I am seeking she who was
I issue from my childhood and thus from nowhere else
midnight light   alphabet of nothingness

Sea of the setting sun   white Sea
west of our dreams   vast inner Sea

Translated by Frank Kazich and the author

from Strata of light

In this place of no shadow
light is trying to
rise again from the ashes of the night

what lies beneath the surface of things
the eye refuses to see

what becomes of the tragic miracle
of the labouring soul

of re-invented memory
that liberates us

from all within us that comes
from night and returns to night

• • •

Words create
other light

sometimes the poem shines
with its own radiance

for light
we work with light

Translated by James Kirkup

Hilmy Salem

Hilmy Salem was born in Egypt in 1951. He lives in Cairo, and is editor of the literary magazine *Adab wa Naqd* [Literature and Criticism]. He has published five collections of poetry.

from One step behind the dancers

Most probably we managed to,
for we rocked him in the paper boat,
until the water became a shattering evidence.
But we could scream all right,
before the belle who despises rituals
could feel that the endings of the feather-light
sea are brighter than its beginnings,
and that the meek usually expose their claws
whenever love exceeds
their weight-lifting abilities.

Roofs did not collapse like silence,
for peace is fast asleep on the clothes sight,
and we're both capable of collective screaming
since the day a woman asked a man
not to hold her accountable for her death
without consulting the lawyers.

The passers-by didn't see us when we
sustained the pardon.
We can, then, teach the young generation
true geography.

• • •

"Egyptian railways were second
to be laid out in the whole world,"

the teacher said.
It follows, then, that she pressed her thighs
together, so she could pensively
watch the rice fields,
relieved from the pressure of fantasy.
And when the nipples betrayed her
with an unexpected awakening,
she examined the hair she'd combed
in the night-cabin,
so the captive could dishevel it
with an occasional sigh.
She summoned the criers back to the cabin,
for the soda water was allergic to lips,
and didn't pay the VAT that much
attention, thinking that travelling
such distances toward the immigrants
was the duty of only the disassembled,
those who hadn't paid the mother tax.

Egyptian railways:
a giant leap
towards the flesh.

• • •

She had no idea the flute of nests
would fall upon her
from a place totally unexpected by
trustworthy people.
She then chose the organ instead,
as an indicator of the pit.
But as speed was picked up,
she noticed that the passengers
caught her looking at the conductor
on the sly,
so she wouldn't be betrayed
by the agony of composers who'd
spoiled the cotton dolls
before they stole the spinning-wheel.

The railway press rolled
and printed David's ticket
into the banished woman's handbag,
now that the iodine that
awakened the instincts
would be employed to convince
the parents they're off to the beach,
and that a woman said:
"I'm richer than the sea,"
though she wasn't sure
the hips would be able to prove
her claims right.

Qanawi didn't watch her
'cause no one pointed the scars out,
and she'll make her own breakfast
when the morning comes, and sweep
the balcony. And she knows that
this is the look which brought about
the kissing-of-the-buttocks dispute,
while the switch workers understand
the hard-ons of the sidetracks.

You have no parcels to deliver;
all you have is this:
a female hostage seeking her mate,
tangled up in the fuel's generosity.

Translated by Anton Shammas

Abdulilah Salhi

Abdulilah Salhi was born in 1968 in Beni Milal, Morocco. Since 1990 he has lived in Bordeaux and Paris. He established a literary magazine, *Israf*, with Jalal Hakmaoui, and writes poetry in Arabic and French. Since 1987 his poems have been published in several magazines, notably *La revue perpendiculaire*. He works for the Arabic section of Radio Monte Carlo, Paris.

Words of a nincompoop

I've always only half-understood things.
and that never did any harm
to walls and security measures.
Hangover that state of sober liberty,
more and more resembles occupied territory.
In the middle of the floor the empty bottle
overflows with meaning
and is fairly honest-looking.

I am the incompleted
the jammed alarm
the sobbing and its statue
the diarrhoea putting the tin hat on escape.

I retreat directly
I am tactfully afraid
I inhabit the south of my laughter
and I've less ability to put up with you.

Your flesh is inexact
just like the past
it lacks an index
and a proper contents list.

I detest nitwits who say it's not their century

I'm thirty and it's getting hard
to make it with 20-year-old chicks.
Well, always excepting the plain Janes
and those I treat myself to
for the price of a fix.

I don't have enough dough, right?
to make an impression on those
lofty souls with the skins of birds.
I'm brown, one metre seventy,
sometimes I'm taken for an Arab
on account of my complexion
in such cases the fall-out's considerable.
I like rap and techno
I've tried hard to like Ferrara
and Tarantino.
I take after this century's tail-end
and I'm seriously contemplating
a subscription to a porno mag.

I drink all the time
being hungover is no worse
than any study group.
When I'm making it with a bit of all right
I start writing good poetry
with fewer tears
fewer metaphors
less beauty
less poetry.

When the girls you fancy
are less and less accessible,
you have no other choice –
you have to write better. And better.

Getting the hell out of it

We were men
and we failed to prove it
opportunities fizzled out
and often changed costumes
or numbers.

Men –
we are still men on paper
somewhere at the bottom of the page
between brackets
with our Greek sandwiches
and an urgent need not to forget anything.
Sex, alas,
remains a high sincerity zone.

Confusing "he" and "she" makes them
laugh and brings you some attention
we look for ourselves in porno shots
we do it our own way
to perfection.

There are days when we feel such miserable slobs
putting more sugar in our coffees
making more concessions.
No, you don't get on my tripe, Farid
I'll gladly stand you a beer
talk with you about shit and publishing.
You are so naked
you can't be seen by anybody

instead of snoring,
your pain should adapt itself
to a new kind of escalator.

Translated from the French by James Kirkup

Sadiq al-Sayegh

Sadiq al-Sayegh was born in 1936 in Baghdad. He worked in television and radio, producing and presenting arts and documentary programmes for Iraqi television, and published his poetry and essays in Iraqi and Arab magazines. In 1967 he gained an MA in English and Czech literature from Charles University, Prague. Later he edited arts and literary magazines, among them *al-Fanoon* and *al-Badeel*. He left Iraq in 1979 and settled in London, where he lives now. He has published three collections of his poetry, and is an accomplished calligrapher.

With all your mistakes

It often happens
that you wander
throughout the house
like a restless inner
      flame
  a ticking clock
  an animal with a caged
      soul
thinking of things
      that can only confuse
Blood refrigeration
Heated air
A stroke

  But relax
  Calm down   Keep quiet
How similar you are
    to a whitish
      smoky liquid
    liable if activated
    by the senses
      and a random spark
      to explode
    with all your mistakes

The decay of facts

He told her:
I am no longer
the same person, Eve.

Nowadays
I prefer my blindness
to anything else.

He told her:
Forget the story
of Adam and Eve
Forget everything

And lastly, he said:
It's better
that I kill you, Eve
Adam was not murdered
by the apple

but by the decay
of facts

The wolf

You always said
Don't let the wolf
into your garden
He will antagonise
the hungry moon
behind the clouds
against you while
he licks your wounds

And yet
you did precisely

that which was forbidden
citing your circumstances
as an excuse
blaming the ghost
that never existed
the clock that didn't strike
and mist blocking
your way

You opened the gate
and let the hungry moon
lick your wounds
while it set
other wolves from
behind the clouds upon you

From place to place

To Badr Shakir Al-Sayyab

We will hear still
the water fall
where there are
neither faucets
nor jars

We will hear
the black cats miaow
in the pitch-dark
as they drag
the ventricles of
        the heart
in their claws
from place to place

Translated by Sargon Boulus

Hashim Shafiq

Hashim Shafiq was born in Iraq in 1950. He published his first collection of poems in Baghdad in 1973 where he was working as a journalist. He left Iraq in 1978 for Paris, later living and working in Beirut, Damascus and Nicosia until 1989 when he settled in London. He has published eleven volumes of poetry to date. He has also edited a selection of Iraqi poetry (Aden, 1984), and published one novel (Beirut, 1992). Many of his poems have been translated and published in English, French, German, Italian and Polish anthologies.

Wires

They fenced the house
then the garden.
They surrounded the fence with barbed wire
and chards of broken bottles.
Here they placed bull horns on the door
and a horse hoof on the front step,
and there were spells
and yellow beads –
African rue
and frankincense rising
from humid rooms.
No shadows
on the twisted stairway.
No air
wafting from the dim skyhole.
All that
was a penance,
something like a pledge
to exorcise delusions and suspicions
of an absent beauty.

When at night

When I was a child
my nurse rocked me
and said: my child, sleep here
on the gazelle's forearm
and don't turn to the lightning
where the echoes maunder
When I passed boyhood
I was exempted from callings
and I aged quickly
and lived in misery
and I slept on pavements
my shelter receding from me
my desires vanishing quickly
quickly unfolding
like a woman's handkerchief
a speck of whiteness
in the dark of night

Doubts

A man passed by
He tripped on his shadow
and thought it was a dagger
A woman passes now
she bends on the pavement to a star
She thinks it's a penny
A poet passed by words and coloured them
and thought they were beads
In Iraq a murderer once walked through night
and imagined it was a dagger
and that it would stab him
here here and here

Living

I lived in a raisin cloud
and shook hands with mountains
and was dumbfounded by light
when it touched the whiteness of stone.
This is how I lived
sharing in the sky the life of hawks
and when I landed on earth
someone blocked me
as I walked in the direction of my daily bread!

Affiliation

When I had a room
under the waves of the sea
I belonged to the water's race.
The sands became my people,
the waves my nationality,
the pebbles my blood-kin,
and among weeds I had acquaintances and friends.
That's why I have become a slave
to all that drips and flows,
to each rushing murmur
cleansed by the air.

Firewood speech

There the almond sky
and the morning of grapes
and my mother's clay oven
crowning breakfast loaves
baking the hens' eggs in a realm
fenced by the shadows of dusk.
I was lying behind the oven's clay

tossing to the fire
the questions of dried palm fronds
and the speech of firewood.
There I had a tempting sip,
Ceylon tea boiling
rising in a cloud to a samovar
of silver or gold.

The wall

For each lonely king
for each divorced woman
for each messiah with wood or cross
a wall
with whom he talks
and argues
and sleeps.
In the morning he greets it
when he departs.
And in the evening when he returns
he asks it, stone . . . by stone,
>   *My sir, my dear wall*
>   *will there be a time without masks?*

Translated by Khaled Mattawa

Fadhil Sultani

Fadhil Sultani was born in Iraq in 1948, and left the country in 1977, settling in London. His poetry has been published in several literary magazines, and he writes for *al-Sharq al-Awsat* newspaper in London. He has translated into Arabic William Trevor's collection of short stories *The Ballroom of Romance*, *The Bluest Eye* by Toni Morrison, and more than 25 British poets, including R.S. Thomas, Ted Hughes, Kathleen Raine, Philip Larkin, Dylan Thomas and Kingsley Amis.

The statue

From dawn till sleep
wanderers pass by you.
– where did they all go?
From dawn till sleep
grass grows beneath you
and dust grows on your shoulders.
What remains of you?
Your fingers overlook the wanderers
and a shadow overlooks you.

Dream

Sometimes I dream
of doing what Ibn al-Farid did in the souqs
when desire stormed his body
and the music blew away his turban
and the rhythm stripped him naked –
even to his genitals,
and his skin was transparent
but he saw nothing
except his image in his image.

from Ama-ar-gi

They go, light in spirit, light on feet,
wanderers, sons of devils, ascetic,
carrying some carpets of love,
a piece of sack
some clothes, and dust.
They neither built a house nor left any shadows
they were fractures of fractures
tired from the shivering of their bodies between death and
    death,
from the sun's break-up beneath the earth.
Destruction has prevailed.
Sleep, my little child,
a god will pass me,
a god has just passed me.
The sun rises to touch my forehead.
We walked in the sun,
then we poured a stream upon you,
then we saw you
crossing the earth slightly.
Sleep, my little child,
a god will pass me
a god has just passed me,
caressed my hair and slept in my bed.
Who are you?
A back door that cannot keep out the windstorm?
A water skin that leaks water?
A fireplace where fire dies?
You are the house that collapsed on its inhabitants.
You are the fence between the sky and my face.
Since those engravings,
        those chains,
        those bridges,
        'hose sublime plants,
        ₋nd those date palms,
Ama-ar-gi
O freedom,

do you recognise your Sumerian name?
Be naked,
daughter of my flesh and bones
and may you bathe in the fountain.
In the pure fountain may you bathe.
Let all worshippers come to watch you,
the ten suras,
let the wind come to enter into you.
No wind will be left but to storm you
No sand will be left, but to turn green within you
No death will be left, but to be reborn within you
Creatures! May you come, all, with your clothes,
the daughter of my flesh and bones is naked in the pure
    fountain.
The sun roared
the earth shook beneath me,
I was alone, standing alone.
His face was sad as my hands.
My hands became birds.
Come, son of my mother and my bones,
I made a bed as wide as the Euphrates.
Your name, my love, is raised so high,
I expose it to the sun, and the plants green
I expose it to the wind, and the water dances
I expose it to the sea, and the harbour rejoices.
Lead me to sleep
the day was as long as your shadow on the wall
the evening was as heavy as your step on the strange earth
Lead me to sleep,
my heart is sad,
and all creatures sleep.

Translated by the author
with thanks to Richard McKane

Mubarak Wassat

Mubarak Wassat was born in 1955 in al-Youssefiya, Morocco. He has published one collection of poems, with a second and third being published this year. He has translated many French authors into Arabic. He teaches philosophy in Agadir.

Biography for a withered rose

The lights are pale on the lilac stalks
the steps are crashed on the pavements.
The waves are still, on both sides of the garden.
Nothing is changed
since you deserted this window
this room where the sparrow is laughing
where the water lives and thinks
and the vase is weighed down with its metal insomnia.
Still your broken glance and your jangling bracelets
your scarf and your violet stutter
lie scattered on the sheets crammed with your fright
and on the ink-spattered table
the statue of the fat Buddha laughs merrily –
unfortunately I couldn't look hopeless.

I am as a barren hymn, as an ancient stream,
for details of surprise were achieved without me
for my breath stammers in the void
in spite of the cloud billowing with bloodshot eyes
and snow falls from the ceiling
and plays in my lap like a baby.

Nothing is changed
the murmuring of the broom flows deep into the far
    meadows
the sky that sprinkles drizzles of delirium
while you are getting rid of your blood and running

between the ailing cedar trees
and on roadsides filled with the pain of music.
A rainbow stumbled over a terrorised waist or haunch
and foam repeated the ocean's dreams
your dreams were following you
as whispers and chat thrilled you
and in mid-sentence you disappeared
leaving your petty worries on the doorsteps of hotels
leaving your spectre in the mirror
your face in the new wheat ears
your blue seconds in the golden heart of a watch.

Nothing is changed
your shiver slips through the holes in lace
your fearfulness covers my brow
and I invent a biography for a withered rose
to tell it to an empty nook
to a broken candlestick
before I put my hand on the key of the relationship
while my head is outside the hall of joy
before I sink my eyes into the wet pillow
studded with your sleep and your fragrance
listening to the swamp moss
as it grows in my breast
in this melancholic room
like the smile of a murdered man
where the time is always midnight.

Translated by Noel Abdulahad

Abdo Wazen

Abdo Wazen was born in Beirut in 1957. He studied Arabic litera-
ture at the Lebanese University and at the Saint Joseph University in
Lebanon. Since 1979 he has worked as an arts affairs journalist. He
belongs to the generation of war poets who emerged in the 1980s. He
has published six collections of poetry, one of them *Hadiqat al-Hawas*
[Garden of Sensation] banned on grounds of immorality. He trans-
lated from French into Arabic works by Nadia Tuémiand, Jacques
Prévert, Samuel Beckett's *Waiting for Godot* and Antoine de Saint-
Exupéry's *The Little Prince*. In 1998, he edited and introduced a new
edition of the work of *al-Hallaj*, the Arab mystic (d. 992). He is now
cultural editor of *al-Hayat* daily newspaper in Beirut.

The rare sky

Those who lay in the open
How could they bear the cold
Of a night unlit by a single star?

Those who closed their eyes
– not to see their shadows fade like clouds,
How were they taken unawares by the desolation of the
    seasons
In the middle of their years?

They are the strangers
Gone before lightning could scorch their faces.
They haven't yet defined
The direction of their steps.
They roamed looking for phantoms they lose every night
In the biting cold of their rare skies.

Ophelia

The drowned maiden did not relate tales of the deep
As water carried her body like a flower.
A light dawned in her puzzled eyes,
She was quiescent without distress; without memories,
Her face white like the morn.
When they lifted her, shells and jewels from her silence fell;
From her spread hands rose the cry of a waning moon.

Window of the night

When we looked at the moon
It was steeping hills and meadows in its silence
Its silver spread warmth across the sky,
A sky which did not shade us enough.
The moon does not listen to our coo
But sends us jewelry and fruit.
Every time we fall into its nets,
We exude oil and linden.
Thus does the moon remain
A window for the night,
For our looks that dare not cross their enchanted forest.

Darkness

Night is the beginning of the world!
See how darkness fell over me,
How did a star ripen in my hands?

Night is the end of the world!
See how I stand like a wakeful tree
How do I cross through the doors of sleep?

The strangers' lantern

The sky does not wait for the strangers
If they're late for its banquet.
They wait at the threshold, counting their wounds
Like branches counting their leaves.

In the desolation of the road, the strangers sit
Waiting for a star – or maybe rain,
Until they see the first glimpse of light
That will quench the bewilderment in their eyes
And let them travel on to the night's end.

Strangers do not need a tree
Nor a prayer to accompany them –
No matter how long their road,
It will end in the woods of their dreams.

Coincidence

Who told the flower to wake from the slumber of the tree,
And the bird to rise from the coma of the skies?
Who asked the dove about its murky past?

The flower was but an old wound,
The bird an arrow of morning;
The dove the first shoot of the earth.

Dining table

We stood, silent, before the dining table.
Those we invited did not come,
and the strangers who come unexpectedly did not come.
He whose hand broke the bread
Did not visit us either.

The cup was empty just as our faces.
That night, nobody passed by.
In our hands thorns thrived
And we awaited the first glimpse of light.
Perhaps the visitor knocks,
Perhaps the stranger be guided to our passion stone.

Listening

Never does he sit but to listen,
Never does he stand at the window but to bid the cloud of
    his whims farewell,
Never does he look in the mirror but to see the face he had
    before.

Here is the mysterious man:
Never does he close his eyes but to wake the tree in slumber
    within;
Never does he stop talking but to listen to the sound of a
    rose or dove.

Absence

Here is the door – yet unopened.
The visitors who used to knock again and again
Have not returned from their garden of absence.
Traces of passers-by have vanished into the air,
But many a path is still heard.

Here is the door – not yet shut.
Behind it a strange sun rises,
Behind it sparkle the treasures of the night.

Hidden passion

The blueness I thought was a sea
Was but the memory of your hands.

The blueness that sneaked into your eyes
Was but distress unfamiliar to the skies.

The blueness that preceded your sleep
Is the well of your agony,
Is the kernel of your hidden passion.

Hymn

The angel who knocked at the window by night
Left but a little of the wounds of his palms and the holy
    water,
When we opened the window for him
The freshness of his fingers was still on the panes.

We gathered the incense of his bafflement
From the cold glass
And the angel on whom we had closed our eyes
Was soon as radiant as the hymn of morning.

Translated by Najwa Nasr

Sa'adi Youssef

Sa'adi Youssef was born in Basra, Iraq, in 1934. He was educated in Basra and Baghdad, and worked in teaching and literary journalism. In 1958 he published his fourth, now-renowned, collection, *51 poems*, following the overthrow of the monarchy in Iraq. In the late sixties and seventies he lived in Algeria. Then in 1979 he left Iraq and lived in Syria, Lebanon, France and Jordan. He has published numerous collections of poetry, a volume of short stories, two novels, and essays, and has received several literary awards. His complete poems have been published recently in Beirut. His translations from English into Arabic of international poets, including Walt Whitman, Cavafy, Ritsos, Lorca, Vasco Popa and Ungaretti, also novels by Ngugi wa Thiongo, Wole Soyinka, David Malouf and George Orwell have also been published. His poetry has been translated into several languages, including French, latterly a selection from his collected poems, *Loin du premier ciel*, Actes Sud, Paris, 1999. Sa'adi Youssef now lives in London.

Reception

Snow falls on the cacti, then a cry and a café, a star and encampments, a saint's gown rent by wolves, shoes made of fine leather. How do turtles shiver on the shores of Hadramout? The full moon moans from the bottom of the river . . . and the girls scream in rapture. I do not need a bullet. My only fortune in this world is the wall behind my back. How green the grass on the steppes of Shahrazour! I saw a rope being dangled. Where is Youssef? I was in the markets of Timbuktu . . . and I laboured. One night a ship sailed us through the shoals of Djibouti . . .

Mogadishu tosses lamb's meat to the sharks. I have no destination. I have a cat who lately has begun to tell me the story of my life. Eternity ever receding, why have you too betrayed me? This afternoon I will learn to sip the brutality of flowers. What does treachery taste like? Once I travelled taken

by my song. The soldiers' trains roll on . . . rolling. Roll on.
Rolling. Roll on. Rolling . . . The snow of Moscow warms my
tears. There is no virtue to herdsmen as they settle and as they
set for travel . . . Cities dissolve villages with the shake of a
finger. My bread is made of coarse rice flour, and the salt of
my fish is ash. There is no chance I will be her lover tonight in
the girls' dormitory. No . . . On Saturdays she closes her door
to me. I will burn the papers. The police officer may arrive. On
the night train I dozed off in my chains. And the wooden seat
was my plane that crashed. They are chanting for you, girl of
the harbour tavern. The strangers returned from their search
for diamonds. On the stone of Hejja the eagles of Hemair take
their rest. Once I almost found the child-moon in my palm.
Why did the people leave the park? I do not want your hand.
Do not toss me your rope made of tatters. Today I have found
another torrent: Welcome to life . . . welcome, my other lover.

Amman, 23 March 1997

America, America

> *God save America*
> *My home sweet home!*

The French general who raised his tricolour
over Nagrat al-Salman where I was a prisoner thirty years
    ago . . .
in the middle of that U-turn
that split the back of the Iraqi army,
the general who loved St Emilion wines
called Nagrat al-Salman a fort . . .
Of the surface of the earth, generals know only two
    dimensions:
whatever rises is a fort
whatever spreads is a battlefield.
How ignorant the general was!
But *Liberation* was better versed in topography.

The Iraqi boy who conquered her front page
sat carbonised behind a steering wheel
on the Kuwait–Safwan highway
while television cameras
(the booty of the defeated and their identity)
were safe in the truck like a storefront
on rue de Rivoli.
The neutron bomb is highly intelligent,
it distinguishes between
an "I" and an "Identity".

> *God save America*
> *My home sweet home!*

> *Blues*

How long must I walk to Sacramento
How long will I walk to reach my home
How long will I walk to reach my girl
How long must I walk to Sacramento
For two days, no boat has sailed this stream
two days, two days, two days
Honey, how can I ride?
I know this stream
but, O but, O but, for two days
no boat has sailed this stream

La L La La L La
La L La La L La
A stranger gets scared
Don't fear dear horse
Don't fear the wolves of the wild
Don't fear for the land is my land
La L La La L La
La L La La L La
A stranger gets scared

> *God save America*
> *My home sweet home!*

I too love jeans and jazz and *Treasure Island*
and Long John Silver's parrot and the terraces of New
    Orleans
I love Mark Twain and the Mississippi steamboats and
    Abraham Lincoln's dogs
I love the fields of wheat and corn and the smell of Virginia
    tobacco.
But I am not American. Is that enough for the Phantom pilot
    to turn me back to the Stone Age!
I need neither oil, nor America herself, neither the elephant
    nor the donkey.
Leave me, pilot, leave my house roofed with palm fronds
    and this wooden bridge.
I need neither your Golden Gate nor your skyscrapers.
I need the village not New York.
Why did you come to me from your Nevada desert, soldier
    armed to the teeth?
Why did you come all the way to distant Basra where fish
    used to swim by our doorsteps.
Pigs do not forage here. I only have these water buffaloes
    lazily chewing on water lilies.
Leave me alone soldier.
Leave me my floating cane hut and my fishing spear.
Leave me my migrating birds and the green plumes.
Take your roaring iron birds and your Tomahawk missiles. I
    am not your foe.
I am the one who wades up to the knees in rice paddies.
Leave me to my curse.
I do not need your day of doom.

> *God save America*
> *My home sweet home!*

America
let us exchange your gifts.
Take your smuggled cigarettes
and give us potatoes.
Take James Bond's golden pistol
and give us Marilyn Monroe's giggle.
Take the heroin syringe under the tree

and give us vaccines.
Take your blueprints for model penitentiaries
and give us village homes.
Take the books of your missionaries
and give us paper for poems to defame you.
Take what you do not have
and give us what we have.
Take the stripes of your flag
and give us the stars.

Take the Afghani Mujahedin's beard
and give us Walt Whitman's beard filled with butterflies.
Take Saddam Hussain
and give us Abraham Lincoln
or give us no one.

Now as I look across the balcony
across the summer sky, the summery summer
Damascus spins, dizzied among television aerials
then it sinks, deeply, in the stories of the forts
                              and towers
                                 and the arabesques of ivory
and sinks, deeply, from Rukn al-Din
then disappears from the balcony.

And now
I remember trees:
the date palm of our mosque in Basra, at the end of Basra
the bird's beak
and a child's secret
a summer feast.
I remember the date palm.
I touch it. I become it, when it falls black without fronds
when a dam fell hewn by lightning.
And I remember the mighty mulberry
when it rumbled, butchered with an axe . . .
to fill the stream with leaves
and birds
and angels
and green blood.

I remember when pomegranate blossoms covered the
    pavements,
the students were leading the workers' parade . . .

The trees die
pummelled
dizzied,
not standing
the trees die.

> *God save America*
> *My home sweet home!*

We are not hostages, America
and your soldiers are not God's soldiers . . .
We are the poor ones, ours is the earth of the drowned gods
the gods of bulls
the gods of fires
the gods of sorrows that intertwine clay and blood in a song.
  . .
We are the poor, ours is the god of the poor
who emerges out of the farmers' ribs
hungry
and bright
and raises heads up high . . .
America, we are the dead
Let your soldiers come
Whoever kills a man, let him resurrect him
We are the drowned ones, dear lady

We are the drowned
Let the water come

Damascus, 20 August 1995

The hermit

1

The poets leave
one after the other, at the end of the night.
They carried nothing but a poor man's provisions
and open return tickets.
I tell them: "Do not quicken your steps.
Brothers, wait another hour.
We are at the end of the night."
But they leave.

The sky is not pitch black. Only clouds fall deeply . . .
Black, they seem, and grey. Dawn is leery, yet it is still dawn.
To a constant white cloud in the corner of the sky I say:

I am yours, my crescent-shaped radiance. I waited for you
all night while you were under my pillow, pulling at my
hairs and caressing. You will stay with me.
Wherever I am, you will be. I will tell the sky to clear.
I will proclaim you daylight.
Good morning, dear boy.

2

The poets leave
one after the other, at the end of a verse . . .
How did you end up at point zero?
How did you end up here?
Where did you leave our lanterns, the mountain tops?
Have you never watched the eyes of cats?
Have we followed a line to its end?
Yet, you still leave.

This mountain will not be hemmed. This mountain we
know. From its shacks we will bring honey, and eagle
droppings. The flowers are without names.

And the threadbare spring, and the wolves that sniff for
village smells. There are passageways, the paths of goats

and smugglers. The soldiers are not guests here. The saint's grave is blessed with green ribbons. And from houses we do not know, women and children come with candles and bread.

Good morning, dear mountains!

3

The poets leave
one after the other at the end of a branch.
No:
How can you leave me?
Did we not gather around tables of drink?
How can we say: The ripples on the water are ours.
How can we say: The branches are ours, and the golden
   autumn.
And say: The beginning of the branch.
Yet you leave.

Tree, you are blessed. Flowering, you are blessed with peacock feathers and a hoopoe's crest. You are sacred where ants lay their eggs. The porcupine circles you following the star, and from your branches grasshoppers chirp. In silvery white night you fan yourself with air from paradise. And in golden daylight you distil silver. I will say: you are my first tree. My hut and my tomb, and the crown I wear.

Good morning, poetry!

4

I will not blame you
I will not say goodbye through the wasteland of alcohol,
I will not bend when the storm erupts
I will repeat your names . . .
and your skies.
I will be the trusted guard over what you left behind.
I will be the prince of dust.

5

At night
at the end of the night
birds will come to me

and the prairie wolves will come wet with dew
and the gazelle will come

At the end of the night
seven poets will take refuge in my cave . . .

Amman, 29 November 1994

Translated by Khaled Mattawa

A woman

How will I drag my feet to her now?
In which land will I see her
and on which street of what city
should I ask about her?
– and if I find her house
(Let's suppose I do)
will I ring the bell?
How should I answer?
And how will I stare at her face
as I touch the light wine
seeping between her fingers
How should I say hello . . .
and how will I take the pain of all these years?
Once –
twenty years ago –
in an air-conditioned train
I kissed her all night through . . .

8 September 1994

Translated by the author and Khaled Mattawa

Abdallah Zreka

Abdallah Zreka was born in Casablanca in 1953. He graduated in sociology from Rabat College of Humanities. He published his first collection of poetry in 1977, five between 1981 and 1995, and two novels between 1991 and 1998. Three collections were published in French between 1982 and 1998, and individual poems have appeared in a number of international anthologies. He lives in Casablanca.

from Black candle drops

1

And so I snuffed
the candle out to light up the dark

and saw the sun
separated from its light

and saw doors
but couldn't see a land

Butterflies crawled
out of the worms in dead bodies

I was afraid
my face was another's
glued to mine

and was terrified to see
scorpions under my foot

When I reached water
I sought a mouth in the earth

I saw nothing
but a land similar
to a turtle's carapace

and cried out:
Hell is all that remains
of paradise

Paradise may disappear
The fire stays

My hand alone
remained as I vanished

When I returned
my fingers were
tongues of flame

I said:
Oh, if you knew
night is kinder
to me than the day

I could be gone
my cup – never

And I sang:
O my foot my foot
my foot of pleasure

When the woman came over
I blew the candle out

and called:
Forget your language
let your tongue
chew another speech

and thought of the sun
that never saw me naked

In the forest
I saw the wind
but not the flute

and wrote on air:
Do not sing with the wind

(At night
I saw birds
pecking at nipples only)

and to an ant
I called:
Do not go home
There's a jailer
awaiting you
jangling his keys

In the water
I saw a serpent emerge from my mouth

and saw pitch-black silence
in my sleep
        pitch-black!

2

Give me a cup
to drain this emptiness

And an arm
to measure this separation

Prepare for me
a bed of glass
on which my nightmares may slide

I don't want to read any letters
that won't stand up
like nails to my eyes

I will offer this approaching dog my hand
to bite off a few fingers

And leave a lot of whiteness in my writings
for this whore to trace as she likes

(This is not a pen
but a pickaxe
to demolish this poet
who haunts me)

The ants shall walk in my funeral
I shall leave my grave for someone
who has no place to sleep

and leave a lot of whiteness in my writings
to light up the darkness that comes
with the night of words

I shall leave the white for your wedding day

3

I saw white fleeing from white
and white fleeing from the wall
                              and didn't see

The wall fleeing from the white
earth fleeing the sea
                              and didn't see

The sea fleeing from the whale
The whale fleeing from its skin
                              and didn't see

I saw fear out-race the cold to the ears
The ears out-race the eye to the thing

The thing out-step the name
The name get ahead of the tongue

And the tongue emerge from one mouth
to enter another
                    and didn't see

I saw a doorless room
and a wall eating a woman's leg

a window race an eye
to another eye

a dead woman under a bed
a bed over a living woman

and a naked one on a floor
which was all mirror
                    and didn't see

And I saw a letter in the shape of a man
the line a straight road to hell
the dots were oblivion amid the words
the page a ticket
                    to enter the fire

        And all that I saw
        I have yet to see

Translated by Sargon Boulus

The Translators

NOEL ABDULAHAD is a Palestinian writer, critic, poet and translator who lives in the USA.

JAREER ABU-HAIDAR was born in the Lebanon. He is currently a visiting reader at the School of Oriental and African Studies, University of London. He has published numerous studies, particularly on Hispano-Arabic literature and its possible relations with the Provençal troubadours. His work *Hispano-Arabic Literature and the Early Provençal Lyrics* is published by Curzon Press, London, October 2000.

SEEMA ATALLA *See page 27.*

SARGON BOULUS *See page 70.*

CLAIRE FARAH is a Lebanese translator who lives in Paris.

MARILYN HACKER is a renowned American poet, and translator from the French. She has published several collections of poems. She teaches in New York.

NAY HANNAWY was born and grew up in Lebanon. She has taught Arabic and English at Arkansas University, where she received her MFA in literary translation. In July 1999, her translation of Jabour Douaihy's *Autumn Equinox* won the Arkansas Press Prize for Literary Translation from Arabic. She now lives in Kuwait and teaches English and translation.

ABDULLA AL-HARRASI is an Omani academic and translator. He teaches translation at Sultan Qaboos University in Muscat. Currently he is working on a Ph.D. thesis in translation studies at Aston University in Birmingham, UK. He has published Arabic translations of several literary and academic works from English.

ADNAN HAYDAR is Professor of Arabic and comparative literature at the University of Arkansas. He has co-authored and co-edited several books, translations and interpretations of poetry and fiction and writes on modern literary theory and oral poetry. He has translated three novels, including the translation of Jabra Ibrahim Jabra's *In Search of Walid Masoud*. From 1993-1999 he was director of the King Fahd Middle East Studies Program at the University of

Arkansas. In 1991 he was awarded a Fulbright Senior Research Fellowship in Jordan and the West Bank.

PAULA HAYDAR is a freelance translator and teacher of Arabic at the Lebanese American University. She has published translations of two novels by Lebanese author Elias Khoury with the University of Minnesota Press, and a third, *The Kingdom of Strangers*, with the University of Arkansas, for which she was awarded the American Translators Award for Translation of Arabic Fiction in 1996. She received an NEH Fellowship for translation and, in 1995, the student award for literary translation from the American Translators Association.

NAWAR AL-HASSAN GOLLEY was born in Syria, and has lived, worked and studied in the UK since 1986. She has a first class BA in English and American Studies from Hims University, Syria and a Ph.D. in critical and literary theory from Nottingham University, UK. She worked as a research fellow at the School of Oriental and African Studies in London from 1996 to 1998. Presently she works as an Assistant Professor of English at the American University of Sharjah, United Arab Emirates.

HASSAN HILMY was born in Morocco. He is Professor of English at Hassan II University, Casablanca, where he lives. He translates from Arabic into English and English into Arabic, and has published in Arabic selected poems of W.B. Yeats and a selection of modern American poetry.

JAMES KIRKUP is a poet, novelist, dramatist and translator. He has spent most of his adult life in Europe, Japan and the US, where he has held teaching posts and 'resident writer' positions at several universities. He has written many very personal travel books about Japan, Malaysia, Russia, the Philippines, Korea and the US, and many books of poems on a variety of themes: *No More Hiroshimas*, *A Correct Compassion*, *The Descent into the Cave*, *The Prodigal Son*, *Refusal to Conform*, *The Body Servant*. His latest works are original haiku and tanka as well as translations of these traditional Japanese poetic forms. His *A Book of Tanka* was awarded the Japanese Festival Foundation Prize in 1996, and he won the Scott Moncrieff Prize for literary translation in 1995. He has translated several African authors, including: Camara Laye, Tété-Michel Kpomassie, Aimé Césaire. Kirkup's complete works have been published by the University of Salzburg Press.

SARAH MAGUIRE was born in West London. She has published two collections of poetry, *Spilt Milk* (Secker & Warburg, 1991) and *The Invisible Mender* (Jonathan Cape, 1997). She is well-known for her contributions to BBC radio arts programmes, and also reviews poetry regularly for many British newspapers and journals. She is currently Writer in Residence at the Chelsea Physic Garden, London, and is editing *A Garden Inclosed: The Chatto Book of Botanical Verse*, due out in 2001. She was the first writer/poet to be sent by the British Council to work with writers in both Palestine and Yemen, and collaborated with Peter Clark in translating the poems of Adonis for the Poetry International Festival in London, 1998.

KHALED MATTAWA *See page 156.*

RICHARD MCKANE was born in Melbourne, Australia in 1947. In 1978 he was the first non-US citizen to be awarded the Hodder Fellowship at Princeton University as a writer. He has translated over 20 books from both Russian and Turkish. He published his first collection of poetry in London and New York in 1993, and in 1998 *Poet for Poet*, an anthology of his poems, together with new and selected translations.

IBRAHIM MUHAWI was born in 1937 in Ramallah, Palestine, and was educated there and in the USA. He taught English Literature in Canada, Jordan, Palestine and Tunisia, and was later Professor of Folklore and Rhetoric at the University of California, Berkeley. He now lectures in translation studies at the Department of Islamic and Middle East Studies at the University of Edinburgh. He translated and introduced into English Mahmoud Darwish's *Memory for Forgetfulness* (1995), and is co-author of *Speak Bird, Speak Again: Palestinian Arab Folktales* (English 1988; French 1997).

ANTON SHAMMAS is a Palestinian writer and translator of Arabic, Hebrew and English. His novel *Arabesques* (Hebrew 1986; English 1988 and Penguin International Writers 1990) was chosen by the *New York Times Book Review* as one of the best seven novels of 1988. He is a Professor of Comparative Literature and Near Eastern Studies at the University of Michigan, Ann Arbor, USA, where he has lived since 1987.

Sources and Acknowledgements

The editors and publisher gratefully acknowledge permission to republish poems translated in issues of Banipal *from the following published and unpublished works:*

Hoda Ablan: from *Muhawala li-tathakkur ma hadath* [An Attempt to Remember what Happened] Andiyat al-Fatayat, Sharjah, al-Dar al-Misriya, al-Lubnaniya, Cairo, 1998.

Fawziyya Abu Khalid: from *Ma' al-sarab* [Water of the Mirage], published by Dar al-Jadeed, Beirut, 1995.

Etel Adnan: unpublished prior to appearing in *Banipal*.

Seema Atalla: unpublished prior to appearing in *Banipal*.

Fadhil al-Azzawi: from new and unpublished poems, those published in Arab newpspapers, and from the poet's collections in Arabic and in German.

Basheer al-Baker: from *Qanadeel ila rassif oroppi* [Lamps for a European Pavement], Dar al-Jadeed, Beirut, 1994.

Ahmad Barakat: from *Dafater al-khasran*, Moroccan Union of Writers Publications, Rabat, 1994.

Taha Bekri: excerpt from *Les rêves impatiens*, Editions Hexagone, Montreuil, 1997.

Tahar Ben Jelloun: two poems from *Les Pierres du temps* [The Ephemeral Childhood]; and an excerpt from the beginning of *La remontée des cendres*, Editions du Seuil, Paris, 1991.

Mohammed Bennis: The excerpt from "Hieroglyphics" and "Rose of Dust" are from the collection *Al-makan al-wathani* [The Pagan Place], Editions Toubqal, Casablanca, 1996.

Mohammed Bentalha: from *Ghaima ouw hajar* [Cloud or Stone], Editions Toubqal, Casablanca, 1995.

Abbas Beydhoun: From two collections, *Hujurat*, Dar al-Jadeed, Beirut, 1996, and *Li mareedhin huwa al-amal*, Dar al-Masa, Beirut, 1997.

Faraj Bou al-Isha: from the collection *Ila Fatima kayfama ittafaq*, Dar al-Ardh lil-Nashr, Cyprus, 1993.

Sargon Boulus: "Entries for a possible poem" and "Who knows the story" "are unpublished in Arabic. "Master" and "Remarks to Sindbad from the Old Man of the Sea" are from *Hamil al-fanous fi lail al-dheeab*, Dar al-Jamal, 1996.

Mahmoud Darwish: These translations are from Mahmoud Darwish's penultimate collection, *Sareer al-ghareeba* [Bed of a Stranger], published by Riad el-Rayyes, Beirut, 1999.

Mohammed Dib: These poems are from Dib's latest collection *L'Enfant-jazz*, Editions de la Différence, 1998. French and English versions of the poem "Tree" are carved in granite at Greenwich as part of the Algeria section of the "Poetry on the Meridien Line" display at the Millenium Dome.

Nujum al-Ghanim: from *Rawahil* [Travellers], Dar al-Jadeed, Beirut, 1996.

Qassim Haddad: From the collection *Qaber Qassim*, [Qassim's Grave], published by al-Kalima lil Nashr, Bahrain, 1997; and *Naqd al-amal* [Critique of Hope], published by Dar al-Kunooz al-Adabiya, Beirut, 1998.

Nathalie Handal: unpublished prior to appearing in *Banipal*.

Mohammad al-Harthi: from *Ab'ad min Zinjebar* [Further than Zanzibar], Dar Sharqiyat, Cairo, 1998.

Mohammad Afif al-Hussainy: from the collection *Buhaira min yadayk*, Ala'a Lil Nashr, Paris, 1993.

Abdel Kader El Janabi: "History is always . . . " is from the collection *Marah al-gharba al-sharqiya* [The Mirth of Eastern Alienation], Riad el-Rayyes, 1988; "Every sea . . ." is from *Hayat ma ba'd al-ya* [Living Beyond the Word], Faradis, Paris, 1995; "Willingly, the light" was published in Janabi's French journal, *Homnesie*, No 3, Paris, 1984; "Homage to G. V. Grunebaum" is from the bilingual French and Arabic collection *Nés à Baghdad*, Stavit, Paris, 1997; "Hat Trick . . ." only published in *Banipal* No. 1, February 1998.

Hatif Janabi: from *Faradis, Asakir wa ayail* [Paradises, Deers and Militaries], al-Mada, Damascus, 1998.

Nouri al-Jarrah: These Elegies were published in *al-Hayat* daily newspaper during 1997.

Ahmad Kattouah: from *Kurat suf luffat 'ala 'ajal*, Dar al-Jadeed, Beirut, 1996.

Waleed Khazendar: from the collections *Ghuraf ta'isha*, Dar al-Fikr, Beirut, 1992, and *Satwat al-masa'*, Dar Bissan, Beirut, 1996

Vénus Khoury-Ghata: from the collection *Anthologie personnelle*, Actes Sud, Paris, 1997.

Adel Khuzam: from the collection *al-Wareeth* [The Inheritor], Dar al-Jadeed, Beirut, 1997.

Wafa'a Lamrani : from *Aneen al-a'aly*, Dar al-Adab, Beirut, 1992.

Fatima Mahmoud: from *Ma lam yatayassar*, [Not Available], Tripoli, Libya, 1986.

Salman Masalha: from the collection *Reesh al-bahr* [Sea Feathers], Jerusalem, 1999.

Maram al-Massri: from *Karza hamra' 'ala bilat abyadh* [Red Cherries on White Tiles], Tabr al-Zaman, 1998.

Khaled Mattawa: unpublished prior to apearing in *Banipal*.

Bassem al-Mereiby: from *Thlath majmu'aat* [Three Collections], al-Muassa al-Arabiya lil Dirassat wal-Nashr, Beirut, 1997.

Dunya Mikhail: unpublished prior to appearing in *Banipal*.

Zakaria Mohammed: from the collections *al-Juad yajtoz askadar* [The Horse Passes Askadar], Sorah Publications, London 1994, and *Ashghal yadawiya* [*Artefacts*], Riad el-Rayyes, London, 1990.

Adnan Mohsen: from *La Mémoire du silence*, Editions de l'Harmattan, Paris, 1994. Illustrations by Ali Fenjan.

Amel Moussa: from *Untha al-ma'* [Female of Water], Cérès Editions, Tunis, 1997.

Saadia Mufarreh: from *Mujarrad mir'at mustalqiya* [Merely a Mirror Lying Back], Dar al-Mada, Damascus, 1999.

Khaled Najar: from the collection *Qassa'id li ajil al-malak al-dha'a* [Poems for a Lost Angel], Riad el-Rayyes, London, 1990.

Hassan Najmi: from the collection *Hayat saghira*, Editions Toubqal, Casablanca, 1995.

Amjad Nasser: "Sign", "Hope's front", "Three signs on the blind's way" and "Watchtower" are new poems, not yet published in Arabic. "Once upon an evening, in a café", "Bakunin's fish", "Offering" and "Wildernesses" are from the collection *Athar al-'aber* [Traces of a Passer-by], Dar al-Sharqiyyat lil-Nashr wa al-Tawzi', 1995.

Salwa al-Neimi: from *Ghuwayat nafsi*, Dar Sharqiyyat, Cairo, 1996.

Salah Niazi: from *al-Sahil al-mu'allab* [The Canned Neigh], Riad el-Rayyes, 1990.

Mostafa Nissabouri: Excerpt from *"Approche du désertique"* and *"Aube"*, La Parole Peinte series, Editions La Manar, Casablanca, 1999.

Saif al-Rahbi: from the collections: [Mountains] (1996), [A Man from the Empty Quarter] (1994), [One Knife is not Enough to Slaughter a Sparrow] (1988) and [The Traveller's Head] (1986).

Fuad Rifqa: from the collections *Jarrat al-samiri* [The Jar of the Samaritan], Dar Sader, Beirut, 1995 and *Qasa'id hindi ahmar* [Red Indian Poems], Dar Sader, Beirut, 1993.

Wadih Sa'adeh: from *Muhassalat wassl dhiffatain bisawt*, Dar al-Nahar, Beirut, 1997.

Amina Saïd: "I was born on the shores" from the collection *Marcher sur terre*, La Différence, Paris, 1994; two untitled poems from *Gisements de lumière*, La Différence, Paris, 1998.

Hilmy Salem: from *Sarab al-triko* [The T-Shirt Mirage], Cairo 1995.

Abdulilah Salhi: from *Revue Perpendiculaire*, No. 8, Winter 1999.

Hashim Shafiq: from the collection *Taif min khuzaf* [Dream from Pottery], Budapest, 1991, from unpublished works, and from *Mi'at qasida wa qasida* [A Hundred Poems and a Poem], Dar an-Nahar, Beirut, to be published late 2000.

Sadiq al-Sayegh: published in *al-Hayat* daily newspaper.

Fadhil al-Sultani: from a new collection *Muhtariqan bil ma'* [Burned by Water], Al-Kunoos al-Adabiya, Beirut, April 2000.

Mubarak Wassat: from *Ala daraj al-miyah al-'amiqa*, Editions Toubqal, Casablanca, 1990.

Abdo Wazen: from *Abwab al-nawm* [Doors of Sleep], Dar al-Jadeed, Beirut, 1996.

Abdallah Zreka: from the collection *Farrashat sawda'* [Black Butterflies], Editions Toubqal, Casablanca, 1988.